D0515884

CLEOPATRA

◆ ◆ ◆

❖ ANCIENT WORLD LEADERS ❖

❖ ANCIENT WORLD LEADERS ❖

CLEOPATRA

RON MILLER AND SOMMER BROWNING

CHELSEA HOUSE
P U B L I S H E R S
An imprint of Infobase Publishing

Frontis: Cleopatra, the famed Egyptian queen, dissolving a pearl in a glass of wine (some legends say vinegar), which won her a challenge in extravagance against Mark Antony.

Cleopatra

Copyright © 2008 by Infobase Publishing

Chelsea House
An imprint of Infobase Publishing
132 West 31st Street
New York, NY 10001

Library of Congress Cataloging-in-Publication Data

Miller, Ron, 1947–
   Cleopatra / Ron Miller and Sommer Browning.
      p. cm. — (Ancient world leaders)
   Includes bibliographical references and index.
   ISBN-13: 978-0-7910-9582-9 (hardcover) 1. Cleopatra, Queen of Egypt, d. 30 B.C.—Juvenile literature. 2. Egypt—History—332-30 B.C.—Juvenile literature. 3. Queens—Egypt—Biography—Juvenile literature. I. Browning, Sommer. II. Title.
   DT92.7.M55 2008
   932'.021092—dc22   2007050079

Text design by Lina Farinella
Cover design by Jooyoung An

Printed in the United States of America

Bang FOF 10 9 8 7 6 5 4 3 2 1

This book is printed on acid-free paper.

❖ CONTENTS ❖

Arthur M. Schlesinger, Jr.
On Leadership

Leadership, it may be said, is really what makes the world go round. Love no doubt smoothes the passage; but love is a private transaction between consenting adults. Leadership is a public transaction with history. The idea of leadership affirms the capacity of individuals to move, inspire, and mobilize masses of people so that they act together in pursuit of an end. Sometimes leadership serves good purposes, sometimes bad; but whether the end is benign or evil, great leaders are those men and women who leave their personal stamp on history.

Now, the very concept of leadership implies the proposition that individuals can make a difference. This proposition has never been universally accepted. From classical times to the present day, eminent thinkers have regarded individuals as no more than the agents and pawns of larger forces, whether the gods and goddesses of the ancient world or, in the modern era, race, class, nation, the dialectic, the will of the people, the spirit of the times, history itself. Against such forces, the individual dwindles into insignificance.

So contends the thesis of historical determinism. Tolstoy's great novel *War and Peace* offers a famous statement of the case. Why, Tolstoy asked, did millions of men in the Napoleonic Wars, denying their human feelings and their common sense, move back and forth across Europe slaughtering their fellows? "The war," Tolstoy answered, "was bound to happen simply because it was bound to happen." All prior history determined it. As for leaders, they, Tolstoy said, "are but the labels that serve to give a name to an end and, like labels, they have the least possible connection with the event." The greater the leader, "the more conspicuous the inevitability and the predestination of every act he commits." The leader, said Tolstoy, is "the slave of history."

Determinism takes many forms. Marxism is the determinism of class. Nazism the determinism of race. But the idea of men and women as the slaves of history runs athwart the deepest human instincts. Rigid determinism abolishes the idea of human freedom—the assumption of free choice that underlies every move we make, every word we speak, every thought we think. It abolishes the idea of human responsibility, since it is manifestly unfair to reward or punish people for actions that are by definition beyond their control. No one can live consistently by any deterministic creed. The Marxist states prove this themselves by their extreme susceptibility to the cult of leadership.

More than that, history refutes the idea that individuals make no difference. In December 1931 a British politician crossing Fifth Avenue in New York City between 76th and 77th Streets around 10:30 p.m. looked in the wrong direction and was knocked down by an automobile— a moment, he later recalled, of a man aghast, a world aglare: "I do not understand why I was not broken like an eggshell or squashed like a gooseberry." Fourteen months later an American politician, sitting in an open car in Miami, Florida, was fired on by an assassin; the man beside him was hit. Those who believe that individuals make no difference to history might well ponder whether the next two decades would have been the same had Mario Constasino's car killed Winston Churchill in 1931 and Giuseppe Zangara's bullet killed Franklin Roosevelt in 1933. Suppose, in addition, that Lenin had died of typhus in Siberia in 1895 and that Hitler had been killed on the western front in 1916. What would the 20th century have looked like now?

For better or for worse, individuals do make a difference. "The notion that a people can run itself and its affairs anonymously," wrote the philosopher William James, "is now well known to be the silliest of absurdities. Mankind does nothing save through initiatives on the part of inventors, great or small, and imitation by the rest of us—these are the sole factors in human progress. Individuals of genius show the way, and set the patterns, which common people then adopt and follow."

Leadership, James suggests, means leadership in thought as well as in action. In the long run, leaders in thought may well make the greater difference to the world. "The ideas of economists and political philosophers, both when they are right and when they are wrong," wrote John Maynard Keynes, "are more powerful than is commonly understood. Indeed the world is ruled by little else. Practical men, who believe themselves to be quite exempt from any intellectual influences, are usually the slaves of some defunct economist. . . . The power of vested interests is vastly exaggerated compared with the gradual encroachment of ideas."

But, as Woodrow Wilson once said, "Those only are leaders of men, in the general eye, who lead in action. . . . It is at their hands that new thought gets its translation into the crude language of deeds." Leaders in thought often invent in solitude and obscurity, leaving to later generations the tasks of imitation. Leaders in action—the leaders portrayed in this series—have to be effective in their own time.

And they cannot be effective by themselves. They must act in response to the rhythms of their age. Their genius must be adapted, in a phrase from William James, "to the receptivities of the moment." Leaders are useless without followers. "There goes the mob," said the French politician, hearing a clamor in the streets. "I am their leader. I must follow them." Great leaders turn the inchoate emotions of the mob to purposes of their own. They seize on the opportunities of their time, the hopes, fears, frustrations, crises, potentialities. They succeed when events have prepared the way for them, when the community is awaiting to be aroused, when they can provide the clarifying and organizing ideas. Leadership completes the circuit between the individual and the mass and thereby alters history.

It may alter history for better or for worse. Leaders have been responsible for the most extravagant follies and most monstrous crimes that have beset suffering humanity. They have also been vital in such gains as humanity has made in individual freedom, religious and racial tolerance, social justice, and respect for human rights.

There is no sure way to tell in advance who is going to lead for good and who for evil. But a glance at the gallery of men and women in ANCIENT WORLD LEADERS suggests some useful tests.

One test is this: Do leaders lead by force or by persuasion? By command or by consent? Through most of history leadership was exercised by the divine right of authority. The duty of followers was to defer and to obey. "Theirs not to reason why/ Theirs but to do and die." On occasion, as with the so-called enlightened despots of the 18th century in Europe, absolutist leadership was animated by humane purposes. More often, absolutism nourished the passion for domination, land, gold, and conquest and resulted in tyranny.

The great revolution of modern times has been the revolution of equality. "Perhaps no form of government," wrote the British historian James Bryce in his study of the United States, *The American Commonwealth*, "needs great leaders so much as democracy." The idea that all people should be equal in their legal condition has undermined the old structure of authority, hierarchy, and deference. The revolution of equality has had two contrary effects on the nature of leadership. For equality, as Alexis de Tocqueville pointed out in his great study *Democracy in America*, might mean equality in servitude as well as equality in freedom.

"I know of only two methods of establishing equality in the political world," Tocqueville wrote. "Rights must be given to every citizen, or none at all to anyone . . . save one, who is the master of all." There was no middle ground "between the sovereignty of all and the absolute power of one man." In his astonishing prediction of 20th-century totalitarian dictatorship, Tocqueville explained how the revolution of equality could lead to the *Führerprinzip* and more terrible absolutism than the world had ever known.

But when rights are given to every citizen and the sovereignty of all is established, the problem of leadership takes a new form, becomes more exacting than ever before. It is easy to issue commands and enforce them by the rope and the stake, the concentration camp and the *gulag*. It is much harder to use argument and achievement to overcome opposition and win consent. The Founding Fathers of the United States understood the difficulty. They believed that history had given them the opportunity to decide, as Alexander Hamilton wrote in the first Federalist Paper, whether men are indeed capable of basing government on "reflection and choice, or whether they are forever destined to depend . . . on accident and force."

Government by reflection and choice called for a new style of leadership and a new quality of followership. It required leaders to be responsive to popular concerns, and it required followers to be active and informed participants in the process. Democracy does not eliminate emotion from politics; sometimes it fosters demagoguery; but it is confident that, as the greatest of democratic leaders put it, you cannot fool all of the people all of the time. It measures leadership by results and retires those who overreach or falter or fail.

It is true that in the long run despots are measured by results too. But they can postpone the day of judgment, sometimes indefinitely, and in the meantime they can do infinite harm. It is also true that democracy is no guarantee of virtue and intelligence in government, for the voice of the people is not necessarily the voice of God. But democracy, by assuring the right of opposition, offers built-in resistance to the evils inherent in absolutism. As the theologian Reinhold Niebuhr summed it up, "Man's capacity for justice makes democracy possible, but man's inclination to justice makes democracy necessary."

A second test for leadership is the end for which power is sought. When leaders have as their goal the supremacy of a master race or the promotion of totalitarian revolution or the acquisition and exploitation of colonies or the protection of greed and privilege or the preservation of personal power, it is likely that their leadership will do little to advance the cause of humanity. When their goal is the abolition of slavery, the liberation of women, the enlargement of opportunity for the poor and powerless, the extension of equal rights to racial minorities, the defense of the freedoms of expression and opposition, it is likely that their leadership will increase the sum of human liberty and welfare.

Leaders have done great harm to the world. They have also conferred great benefits. You will find both sorts in this series. Even "good" leaders must be regarded with a certain wariness. Leaders are not demigods; they put on their trousers one leg after another just like ordinary mortals. No leader is infallible, and every leader needs to be reminded of this at regular intervals. Irreverence irritates leaders but is their salvation. Unquestioning submission corrupts leaders and demeans followers. Making a cult of a leader is always a mistake. Fortunately, hero worship generates its own antidote. "Every hero," said Emerson, "becomes a bore at last."

The single benefit the great leaders confer is to embolden the rest of us to live according to our own best selves, to be active, insistent, and resolute in affirming our own sense of things. For great leaders attest to the reality of human freedom against the supposed inevitabilities of history. And they attest to the wisdom and power that may lie within the most unlikely of us, which is why Abraham Lincoln remains the supreme example of great leadership. A great leader, said Emerson, exhibits new possibilities to all humanity. "We feed on genius. . . . Great men exist that there may be greater men."

Great leaders, in short, justify themselves by emancipating and empowering their followers. So humanity struggles to master its destiny, remembering with Alexis de Tocqueville: "It is true that around every man a fatal circle is traced beyond which he cannot pass; but within the wide verge of that circle he is powerful and free; as it is with man, so with communities." ◆

1

An Ancient Land and a New Princess

IT WAS JANUARY IN THE YEAR 69 B.C. WHEN THE THIRD DAUGHTER OF Ptolemy XII Auletes, king of Egypt, was born. It had been nearly 1,000 years since the last of the great pharaohs and even longer since the great pyramids had been constructed. By 69 B.C., they were already considered ancient wonders and were the destination of curious tourists. Greek travelers had been visiting Egypt for centuries, such as the historian Herodotus and philosopher Plato, who came to study a culture they regarded as the cradle of civilization. It had already been 600 years since the great days of the Egyptian Empire; the once-great nation had fallen into political chaos and found itself ruled by a succession of foreign invaders before finally falling under the domination of Persia.

The Pharaohs

"Pharaoh" comes from the Egyptian word *per-aa*, meaning "great house," and originally referred to the royal court or the state itself. From the late eighteenth dynasty (1539–1295 B.C.) onward, "per aa" was used to refer to the actual king himself.

The idea of kingship and the divinity of the pharaoh were central to Egyptian society and religion; each pharaoh was considered to be a combination of the divine and the mortal. Reliefs in temples, tombs, and palaces stressed the king's divine birth and his function as a representative of the gods.

Egyptian mythology holds that the first kings literally became gods. No one knows whether these kings actually existed in human form. Only at the end of the predynastic period (5500–3100 B.C.), prior to the unification of Egypt, are there names of rulers we can recognize. Many scholars believe that the first real king of a unified Egypt was Menes, who ruled at about 3100 B.C., though virtually nothing is known about him.

The names of many of the ancient Egyptian pharaohs are famous, such as Hatshepsut, the "woman pharaoh"; Akhenaten, the heretic king who tried to overthrow the ancient religion of Egypt and, in the process, incurred the undying hatred of his people; Tutankhamen, the "Boy King"; and Ramses II, or Ramses the Great. Tutankhamen, the son-in-law of Akhenaten, was only eight years old when he was put into power. King Tut (as he is now often known) restored all the old gods and brought order to the chaos that his father-in-law had created. Ramses the Great—the same Ramses mentioned in Exodus—was one of the most prolific builders of ancient Egypt, creating great monuments such as Abu Simbel, Karnak and the Luxor Temples, the Ramesseum, and many others.

Egypt was occupied by Persia; this country, in turn, had captured the rich but powerless empire from Psammetichus III, the last of the Egyptian pharaohs—for two centuries, absorbing it into its vast empire, draining Egypt of its grain, and taxing its people heavily. Worse, the Persians showed little respect for the ancient traditions of the Egyptian people—fomenting a deep dislike that erupted in a nearly continuous series of rebellions.

The Egyptians suffered so much under the Persians that they gladly welcomed Alexander the Great as a liberator when he marched into Egypt in 332 B.C. Preceded by his formidable reputation as a world conqueror, Alexander had been met by Mazaces, the Persian governor of Egypt. With no army of his own, Mazaces simply handed the kingdom over to Alexander. Alexander then sailed his fleet down the Nile to the traditional capital of Memphis. Even though worn by time, the monuments of Egypt still made an enormous impression on both the Macedonian troops and their 24-year-old leader.

Alexander was hailed as a liberator and anointed as pharaoh in Memphis on November 14, 332 B.C.; the high priest named him "son of the gods," according to a tradition that dated back almost 3,000 years. Alexander further gained the trust of the Egyptians for the respect he showed for their religion. Nevertheless, he appointed Greeks to virtually every major position in the country, making Egypt little more than a colony of Greece. Meanwhile, he created the fabulous port city of Alexandria at the mouth of the Nile. This was to be both the new capital of Egypt and a way station for the siphoning of Egypt's great wealth to Greece, where Alexander needed it to finance his ambitious military campaigns.

Just before Alexander's death in Babylon in 323 B.C., he bequeathed his empire to "the strongest": Among these were Antigonus, the grandson of one of his commanders, who became ruler of Macedonia and Greece; Seleucus, a general who inherited most of the old Persian empire; and Ptolemy, another general and one of Alexander's closest companions, who was given the land of Egypt.

Ptolemy immediately began work to protect his new kingdom from his rivals. The fleet of ships he built commanded

Once of history's greatest leaders and conquerors, Alexander the Great was welcomed into Egypt and made pharaoh because he brought an end to Persian rule.

the Mediterranean. The navy was based in Alexandria, which quickly became a great center of commerce and trade, especially since Ptolemy did all he could to encourage merchants and craftsmen to emigrate there. He established a national bank and erected one of the seven wonders of the ancient world: the great Lighthouse of Alexandria. From its position on the island of Pharos, the light from the 370-foot tower could be seen from miles at sea.

Alexandria was soon one of the richest cities in the world, with goods pouring in from Africa, the British Isles, China, Spain, and India. Its warehouses were crammed with tin, cotton, amber, precious metals, and grains. Not only was it a rich city, it was a beautiful one. Carefully planned by Alexander's engineers, it boasted broad, clean streets that were lit at night. Pedestrians could stroll in safety down covered sidewalks, and

Alexander the Great

Alexander III of Macedonia, better known as Alexander the Great, was born in the northern Greek kingdom of Macedonia in 356 B.C. to Philip II and his formidable wife, Olympias. He was educated by the philosopher Aristotle. Following his father's assassination in 336 B.C., he led his army to victories across the Persian territories of Asia Minor, Syria, and Egypt without incurring a single defeat. By the time he was 25, he had already been named Pharaoh of Egypt and Great King of Persia. Over the next eight years, Alexander created an empire that stretched across three continents and covered some two million square miles. He founded more than 70 cities (many of them modestly named "Alexandria").

This vast territory—stretching from Greece in the west, the Danube River in the north, Egypt in the south, and as far east as India—was united not only by commerce and trade but also by a common Greek language and culture. Unfortunately, Alexander was primarily a soldier rather than a ruler or administrator, and his empire quickly disintegrated during the power struggles of his successors following his death in 323 B.C. at the age of 32.

the city's citizens enjoyed fresh water piped directly to their homes. Stadiums, baths, gymnasiums, and concert halls were freely available to all.

Ptolemy established a museum that consisted of a library containing half a million volumes, lecture rooms, and exhibition halls. Attracting both students and learned men from all over the world who wanted to both learn and teach there, the museum became the world's first true university. The catalog of the library alone consisted of 120 scrolls that were each up to 20 feet long. To all of this, Ptolemy added an observatory where a Greek scientist named Aristarchus determined that the Earth and planets circled the Sun. Here, also, Eratosthenes measured the circumference of the planet.

Alexandria quickly replaced Athens as the seat of Greek science and learning. At the university, students could study astronomy, geography, physics, mathematics, zoology, language, and literature. The children of the Ptolemies (the Ptolemaic dynasty) studied there, as did the children of ordinary citizens, with the result that the royal princes and princesses received the best educations available in the world.

The wealthy inhabitants—including Ptolemy himself and his family—lived in unprecedented luxury. Spacious, airy, well-lit rooms were decorated with fine paintings, carved furniture, and elaborate mosaics on the floors. Ptolemy's own palaces, built of marble and set in the middle of vast gardens, were located on a point of land that formed one side of the city's harbor.

Ptolemy was eager to turn Egypt into a model Grecian colony. Egyptian craftsmen were encouraged to abandon their traditional working methods and adapt those of Greece. Greek was also considered the official language of Egypt. Although all of the Ptolemies were tolerant—and even interested in—Egyptian religion and culture, they never considered the country to be anything other than a subkingdom of Greece. Greek was made the official language, Greeks occupied all positions of authority and power, and Egyptian cities were given new Greek names.

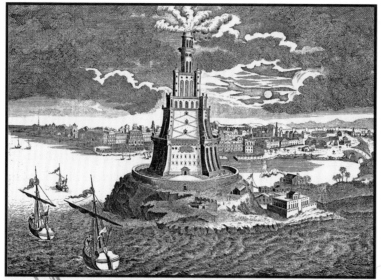

One of the Seven Wonders of the Ancient World, the Pharos Lighthouse of Alexandria was built by Ptolemy, and was completed after twenty years of construction. It was the first lighthouse in the world, and other than the Great Pyramid, the tallest structure in the world at that time.

In fact, "Egypt" itself is a Greek name . . . . the Egyptians had called their country "Kemet." No native Egyptian would again rule Egypt for 1,500 years.

Ptolemy ruled Egypt in the name of Philip III and Alexander IV, the joint kings of Greece. As the empire of Alexander the Great continued to disintegrate, Ptolemy took the title of King in 305 B.C., founding the Ptolemaic dynasty that was to rule Egypt for nearly 300 years—the last ruling family Egypt would ever see.

Ptolemy lived until 283 B.C., and the throne passed on to his son, Ptolemy Philadelphus. He continued the work his father had begun, and Alexandria grew even greater in power and culture, if that were possible. He reconstructed the agricultural industry of Egypt, which had declined under the regimes that had ruled the country between the time of the last pharaohs and the Greeks. In 246 B.C., Ptolemy Philadelphus died and his son, Ptolemy Euergetes, succeeded him. Euergetes added to the extent of Egypt by conquering neighboring regions of Babylonia, while the great fleets of Alexandria conquered the Aegean Sea.

The Ptolemies who followed did not have either the strength, imagination, or ambition the earlier leaders possessed. They failed to maintain the navy and army, and Egypt fell into another long decline. Little by little its land was nibbled away by its enemies until, by the time of the twelfth of the line of Ptolemies, all that was left to rule was the valley of the Nile itself.

This is the world that the daughter of Ptolemy XII inherited. Like all the rulers who had preceded him, Ptolemy XII had taken the name "Ptolemy." Princesses and queens, however, preferred the name Berenice or, like the third daughter of King Ptolemy XII Auletes, Cleopatra.

Cleopatra

IF YOU WERE TO HAPPEN TO SEE CLEOPATRA THEA PHILOPATOR AT A SHOP- ping mall today, you might not give her a second glance. She would not look much different from any other young girl in her early teens. She was a small, petite blonde who was neither particularly beautiful nor particularly homely. Her smooth, oval face was distinguished by large, wide-spaced eyes and a bow-shaped mouth. Her most distinguishing feature, however, was her nose. It was large and curved, like the beak of some predatory bird. It gave to a face that might otherwise have been ordinary, undistinguished, and plain a sense of strength, power, and direction, like the arrow of a weather vane, the needle in a compass—or the prow of a great warship. The great French philosopher Blaise Pascal, once remarked, "If

Cleopatra's nose were shorter, the shape of the world would have been different."

What really made Cleopatra worth a second look was the intelligence that illuminated her face. It more than made up for any lack of classical beauty. There are only a few good depictions of her that remain from her day, but they show the face of a bright, not unattractive, teenage girl. A face that you might find in any high school anywhere . . . . and probably on the honor roll. The historian Plutarch wrote: "Her actual beauty was not in itself so remarkable; it was the impact of her spirit that was irresistible. The attraction of her person, joining with the charm of her conversation and the characteristic qualities of all she said or did, was something bewitching. It was a delight merely to hear the sound of her voice."

The Ptolemies had already been deified—made gods—by Egyptian "cult of the sovereigns," which made any ruler a god automatically. They shared authority with the main god of any local temple. From the moment of her birth, Cleopatra was considered the daughter of a god, and from childhood onward she had all the authority of a goddess.

A day for the teenage Cleopatra began at dawn, as it did for everyone in Alexandria. Although the Ptolemy family had long since become "Egyptianized," adapting many of the ways of Egyptian culture and society, they did not abandon their Grecian and Macedonian roots. Daily life in the palace at Alexandria was probably not very different from daily life among the aristocracy in Athens or Rome.

Greek doctors had for centuries attached great importance to cleanliness, hygiene, and exercise. The palace had luxurious baths for both men and women, equipped with both hot and cold water. Cleopatra did not use soap, however. She might, instead, rub herself all over with olive oil, which she then scraped off with a special tool with a curved blade, called a *strigil*. More likely she used a coarse powder made of sodium carbonate or a lye obtained from wood ash. Most people of her time took their baths just before their evening meal. Although men had started shaving their beards shortly after the time of Alexander, women had long practiced shaving and using depilatories to remove unwanted hair.

Unless a special occasion dictated something more elaborate, Cleopatra probably settled on nothing fancier for her hair

Despite being known as one of the most beautiful women in history, Cleopatra was known more for her intelligence and seductive charm than for her physical appearance. Unlike most females in Egypt, she had the privilege of a private tutor and access to education in Alexandria.

than tying it up on top of her head with a simple ribbon, though by the time she reached her later teens she was more likely to be indulging in the more elaborate hairstyles worn by older women. A portrait bust of Cleopatra in the Graeco Roman Museum of Alexandria depicts Cleopatra with her hair curled and tied in a bun at the back of her head. Perhaps she applied henna to redden her hair as many Egyptians did. Henna was also used by Egyptian women to color their nails, the soles of their feet, and the palms of their hands. Like any young, modern woman, Cleopatra used all sorts of beauty creams, makeup, and perfumes. Ground minerals, such as greenish-black galena, were used as eyeliner, and ochre would tint the lips a rusty color. She may also have used a powder made from white lead to make her skin look paler and extracts of various plants and seaweeds to rouge her lips and cheeks.

She surely had plenty of jewelry: Necklaces, bracelets, earrings, and anklets were all popular. She would have worn bracelets not only around her wrists but around her upper arms as well. Sometimes these were simple bands of gold or silver and sometimes helices that coiled up her arms like snakes. Her ears would have been pierced for earrings, which were most likely simple, decorative studs or tiny, dangling animals. She might have worn a ring around an ankle or calf as well.

Her usual dress would probably not have been much different from that of any upper-class Grecian or Roman girl, which would have consisted of an underdress of soft linen or silk (the *tunica interior*), and a long over robe (*stola*) of the same material. Over these two garments would be worn the *palla*, or draped outer cloak. These might have been dyed bright scarlet, violet, marigold yellow, crocus yellow, hyacinth purple, rust, green, sea green, or blue, with designs worked into them in darker colors.

While indoors, Cleopatra probably went barefoot; when outside the palace or in the streets, she would have worn sandals (*solae*) with soles made of cork, leather, or wood, or, more likely, shoes (*calcei*). Perhaps, as some women did, Cleopatra had her cobbler prepare her shoes in such a way as to make her appear taller. She had a wide choice of colors in her shoes, too, with the leather dyed red, black, white, or yellow.

When she went out, Cleopatra would surely have carried a leaf-shaped fan and perhaps a parasol to protect herself from the intense Egyptian sun. She may have covered her head with a hoodlike fold of her tunic or worn a broad-brimmed straw hat.

But when Cleopatra dressed for state affairs, her costume was very different. Then, Plutarch said, she generally wore "the robe which is sacred to Isis, and she was addressed as the New Isis." These robes, he went on to say, "are variegated in their colors, for her power is concerned with matter which becomes everything and receives everything, light and darkness, fire and water, life and death."

Cleopatra as Isis was a deliberately calculated role. Already venerated as a literal goddess, she chose to take on the persona of Isis because the cult of that goddess had become one of the most popular throughout the Mediterranean—even in imperial Rome itself. Even though of thoroughly Egyptian origin, the cult had gained in popularity—especially among slaves and merchants struggling under the burden of Roman taxes—because of its message of salvation.

But as to just *what* the robes of Isis looked like, no one knows for sure—and there are a lot of possibilities. This description by second-century author Lucius Apuleius of a woman dressed as Isis might give us some idea of how Cleopatra may have looked: "First she had a great abundance of hair, dispersed and scattered about her neck, on the crown of her head she bore many garlands interlaced with flowers, in the middle of her forehead was a compass in the shape of a mirror, resembling the light of the Moon, in one of her hands she held serpents, in the other, blades of corn, her vestment was of fine silk of many colors, sometimes yellow, sometimes rosy, sometimes like flames, and sometimes (which sorely troubled my spirit) dark and obscure, covered with a black robe in the manner of a shield, and pleated in most the

Ancient hieroglyphics, like this one, indicate the kind of wardrobe Cleopatra wore in order to resemble the deities. By modeling herself after the Egyptian goddess Isis, and learning to speak Egyptian, Cleopatra gained popularity with the native people and Isis worshippers.

subtle fashion at the skirts of her garments, the welts appeared comely, whereas here and there the stars glimpsed, and in the middle of them was placed the Moon, which shone like a flame of fire, round about the robe was a coronet or garland made with flowers and fruits. In her right hand she had a timbrel of brass, which gave a pleasant sound, in her left hand she bore a cup of gold, out of the mouth whereof the serpent Aspis lifted up his head, with a swelling throat, her odoriferous feet were covered with shoes interlaced and wrought with victorious palms."

It's possible Cleopatra may have worn something of more conventional Greek or Roman design, but, perhaps because of the special interest she showed in Egypt by learning the language, she opted for a costume that resembled the depictions of Isis in ancient Egyptian wall paintings. This would certainly have endeared her to her Egyptian subjects, many of whom still practiced the old religion and resented the incursion of Greek culture imposed on them by the Ptolemies.

Even though she shared the status of being a god with her brothers and sisters, her ability to speak Egyptian must have set her apart, so far as the Egyptian people were concerned. This allowed her to develop an intimacy with the priests and the native people her siblings were never able to enjoy. It was an intimacy she actively encouraged by taking on the appearance of the popular Egyptian goddess Isis.

Cleopatra's father, Ptolemy XII, probably took his 11-year-old daughter with him when he traveled to Rome in 58 B.C., after passing through Rhodes and Athens. While in Italy, she most likely stayed at one of the villas belonging to Pompey, then the protector of Egypt's interests. There was a great temple there, dedicated to Isis—one of the largest in the world—and Cleopatra almost certainly visited it. At the time, there was a great deal of dissension in Rome regarding the cult of Isis, with only a minority of the Senate being followers of the goddess. The remainder were vehemently opposed and did their best to shut down the temples.

A Game Cleopatra May Have Played

Egyptians from all classes of society enjoyed playing board games, and nearly every Egyptian played Senet. Archaeologists have found over forty Senet boards, many sealed in tombs, and they think it could be the oldest board game in history. No rules for Senet have ever been discovered; historians believe the rules were transferred from player to player by word of mouth. However, with some educated guessing and the help of ancient paintings depicting the game, historians have recreated the rules.

This is a common version of the way historians think Senet was played: The board is divided into 30 squares: 3 rows of 10 squares each. The object of the game is to get all five of your pieces on the board, move them around the board in a backward S shape, and then move all of your pieces off the board. In Egypt, it was usually five cone-shaped pieces pitted against five flat, round pieces. Instead of throwing dice to determine how many squares your piece moves, you throw two-sided "casting sticks." One side of the stick is painted, while the other side is not. The number of sticks that land with the painted side up is the number of spaces your piece moves. Every piece has to get on the board with a throw of the sticks. If you throw a four, for instance, you make it onto the board and place your piece in the fourth square in the top row. You and your opponent alternate throwing the sticks. With each throw, you decide to either move your sticks forward or bring a new piece onto the board, until they are all represented. If the space you want to move into is occupied by your own piece, however, you can't move into it. If the space is occupied by your opponent's piece, you switch positions, setting your opponent back to where your piece was. Now if that isn't complicated enough, the board has a few special squares marked with different symbols. Some of these squares are safe, meaning no one can knock you off the square; others are traps requiring a certain throw of the casting sticks to release you from the square. It is a game of skill and luck, much like the game of backgammon, which some suggest is Senet's modern version.

Cleopatra's diet was probably no different from that of any other upper-class Greek or Egyptian. She would rise in the early dawn and have a light breakfast—probably wheat or barley bread soaked in a little wine, accompanied by figs and olives. The bread might have been baked in loaves or cooked on a griddle, like a pancake or a tortilla. Toward the middle of the day, she would have had a quick lunch and later, in the early evening, a snack. The heaviest meal of the day would usually be held at sunset, or even later, after dark.

Vegetables would have included beans and lentils, which might have been served as a pâté or in soup. The Greek roots of Cleopatra's family would have made them fond of garlic, cheese, and onions. Egypt would have added lettuce and cucumbers to the menu. Meats would have included pork, mutton, and goat. Egypt would have added oxen to the table, as well as such exotic game as antelope, gazelle, porcupine, hare, and fowl, such as quail and crane. All of these would have been boiled, stewed, or roasted. Ducks and hens were kept for both their eggs and meat. While most meats would have been too expensive for the average person to enjoy on anything but religious feast days, the Ptolemies would have eaten whatever they wanted whenever they wanted it.

As a port city, Alexandrians—including the Ptolemies—would have enjoyed an abundance of fish and other seafood. Sardines, anchovies, eels, shellfish, squid, and octopus could be found daily in the markets. Perch, catfish, carp, and mullet were also consumed. These could be bought fresh, smoked, or pickled in brine. If fresh, fish was most often roasted. Food was eaten with the fingers from plates and bowls made of clay or metal. Sometimes flat breads might serve as food holders. Bread would also serve as a napkin for wiping one's fingers and lips (this bread was usually thrown to the family dogs afterward). Wine was a popular drink, as was milk. Wine might be mixed with honey or resinated in the Greek style. Sometimes, aromatic herbs such as thyme, mint, or cinnamon might be added. From the Egyptians, the Ptolemies probably inherited a love for beer, which was an Egyptian invention.

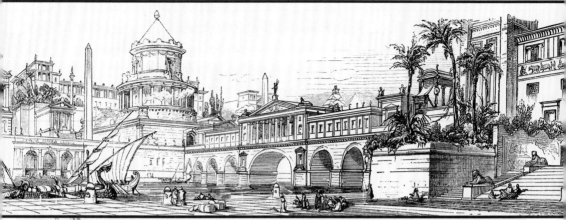

Ancient Alexandria was a hub of knowledge. The first Ptolemy had created the Royal Library of Alexandria and, at one point, it was the largest library in the world. It was here Cleopatra received her education.

Afterward, dessert would consist of such traditional Grecian treats as fresh or dried fruit, figs, raisins, and honey cakes. Since Egypt had been the first land to develop beekeeping, honey was plentiful and would have been an important ingredient in the palace cuisine. Egyptian farmers would have also provided grapes, pomegranates, palm nuts, and almonds.

Cleopatra's father, Ptolemy XII, was neither a particularly commendable human being nor a very good pharaoh, but he had at least one respectable characteristic: he did not stint on his children's education. This was fortunate for Cleopatra and her brothers and sisters, since—although Alexandria and Egypt had declined greatly since the first Ptolemies—the great library and university still existed and were larger and more important than ever. Influential scholars still worked and studied there, and research was constantly ongoing in many different fields of science, philosophy, and art. A girl as intelligent, curious, and ambitious as Cleopatra could not have asked for anything better.

It was not common practice at the time to educate girls and women (there was no proscription *against* women being educated, but they had to do it themselves since they were not typically admitted into schools). However, Cleopatra and her sisters had a distinct advantage: They were all potential rulers of Egypt, and their father—who, if nothing else, inherited a respect for education from the first Ptolemies—deeply appreciated the importance of educating his heirs properly. Each of the six children—boys and girls both—had his or her own personal

The Library of Alexandria

The Royal Library of Alexandria was once the largest library in the world. At first it was part of a great research center, or university, and one of its main jobs, originally, was the editing and copying of texts. It soon became a center for research and learning, and the scholars who worked there came from all over the ancient world.

The library consisted of several buildings. The main book depositories were located near the oldest building, the museum, with a satellite library in the newer Serapeum, which also served as a temple dedicated to Serapis, the Egyptian god of healing (who had been declared the state god by Ptolemy).

According to legend, one of the reasons that the library's collection had grown so large by the time of Ptolemy III was because visitors to the city were required to surrender all books and scrolls in their possession. These were then swiftly copied by official scribes. The originals were retained by the library and the copies given to the owners.

There is no way of knowing exactly how large the library's collection was. It has been a matter of debate among historians for centuries. Although the word "library" suggests a collection of books like this one, it was really a collection of scrolls, which are rolled-up lengths of papyrus. A single work might occupy several scrolls. It is said that King Ptolemy II Philadelphus set a goal of 500,000 scrolls and that Mark Antony donated over 200,000 scrolls to Cleopatra for the library.

tutor. Cleopatra was an avid student who readily absorbed philosophy, mathematics, literature, art, music, and medicine. She eventually learned to write and speak six different languages: Aramaic, Ethiopian, Greek, Hebrew, Latin, and Egyptian. In fact, she was the very first of all the Ptolemies to ever bother to learn the language of the people they ruled. Greek had been the official language not only of the Alexandrine court but of Alexandria as well.

Even if she had not been a good scholar, she could hardly have avoided learning the history of her family and its struggle for power . . . . a struggle that was rapidly losing to the juggernaut of the growing Roman Empire. It was a lesson her brothers and sisters learned as well, all of whom were as anxious to inherit the throne as Cleopatra was. Thus, it was not so much siblings that Cleopatra had as a gang of rivals who, if history were anything to go by, would not let any love for their sister get in their way. She knew that she would eventually be facing a struggle that would be, in every sense, life or death.

One can imagine her looking from the windows of the great library across the sea that lay beyond, toward the distant islands that had once been part of the great Egyptian Empire and which now belonged to Rome: Crete, Lycia, Cyprus, Syria-Coele, and so many others. But what could her father do? For a thousand years, Egypt had had no real army to speak of. For most of that time, the nation had trusted its defense to the hands of its allies and, eventually, the long string of conquerors who had ruled it.

However, so long as her father lived, she could continue her studies and make plans for the future in relative safety. But in 51 B.C., in her seventeenth year, Cleopatra's world changed forever. Her father, Ptolemy XII, died.

CHAPTER

3

A New Queen

PRINCESS CLEOPATRA DID NOT INHERIT A KINGDOM AS MUCH AS SHE
inherited a disaster. To find out just why, we have to take a closer
look at the history of her family, from the time that the second
Ptolemy became the king of Egypt at the age of 25. He was quite
different from his father, Ptolemy I, being much more interested
in intellectual, scientific, and artistic pursuits than in making war.
Although Egypt engaged in numerous wars during his reign, he
left these entirely up to his generals and admirals, taking no
personal interest or part in the battles. Fearful of the increasing
power of Rome, he went out of his way to placate them, such as
sending lavish gifts to celebrate the Roman victory at Pyrrhus. In
return, the Romans sent ambassadors to Alexandria, from which
they returned with so many gifts they felt embarrassed.

His marriage to his sister, Arsinoë II, added to his kingdom the domains that she had earlier acquired independently. The marriage of a brother and sister was commonplace among Egyptian royalty, but it was shocking to Grecian Alexandria. Arsinoë II, who took the surname of Philadelphus ("brother-loving"), was a strong-minded woman who gladly took the reins of power, and a ruthlessly ambitious one who did not hesitate to have inconvenient family members put to death, including Ptolemy's own brother.

Ptolemy II died in 245 B.C. at the age of 63. Ptolemy III, Euergetes I ("the Benefactor") had already taken over the government two years earlier. His surname of "Benefactor" came from his devotion to charitable causes, the arts, and sciences. Unlike his father, however, Ptolemy III was very much interested in military matters. He abandoned his predecessor's policy of keeping out of the wars of the other Greek kingdoms and plunged into the Third Syrian War with the Seleucids of Syria, when his sister, Queen Berenice, and her son were murdered in a dynastic dispute. Ptolemy marched triumphantly into the heart of the Seleucid realm, as far as Babylonia, while his fleets in the Aegean made fresh conquests as far north as Thrace.

This victory marked the zenith of Ptolemaic power. Seleucus II Callinicus kept his throne, but Egyptian fleets controlled most of the coasts of Asia Minor and Greece. After this triumph, Ptolemy III no longer engaged actively in war, although he supported the enemies of Macedonia in the area of Greek politics. His domestic policy differed from his father's in that he patronized the native Egyptian religion more liberally, and he created massive Egyptian monuments that exist to this day. In this, his reign marks the beginning of the gradual "Egyptianization" of the Ptolemies. When Ptolemy III died in 221 B.C., he bequeathed a powerful Egyptian Empire to his son.

During the reigns of Ptolemy II and III, the Egyptian Empire reached its apex, controlling not only Egypt but large expanses of Libya, Israel, Jordan, Lebanon, Syria and Cyprus, parts of Turkey, Thrace and the Peloponnese, and several Aegean islands. Nevertheless, Egypt remained strictly neutral regarding Rome and its mortal enemy, Carthage, not wanting to anger either power.

At about the same time that Ptolemy IV Philoprater ("father-loving") came to the throne, 17-year-old Philip V became King of Macedonia and 18-year-old Antiochus III inherited the Seleucid kingdom. These three young men created a new distribution of power in the Mediterranean—though not to the benefit of Egypt.

Ptolemy IV was, however, a weak and corrupt king under whom the gradual decline of the Ptolemies began. His reign was inaugurated by the murder of his mother, and he was always under the influence of favorites, male and female, who controlled the government. Rebellions by the native Egyptians were signs of the growing weakness of the kingdom. Ptolemy IV was devoted to orgiastic religions and to literature. Much more interested in personal pleasure than in running an empire, he left everything in the unscrupulous hands of his minister, Sosibus. So much under the influence of Sosibus was he that he had his own uncle, brother, and mother killed at the minister's urging. The result of Ptolemy's disinterest and Sosibus's incompetence was a decline in Egypt's army and navy that ended in near disaster when the king of Syria attacked Egypt's Syrian territories. Although Ptolemy IV's forces managed a victory, the invasion triggered a revolt that resulted in the loss of Upper Egypt, a major blow to Ptolemy's income. Since he was no longer able to afford to hire mercenaries for a protective army and navy, he had to cut back on overseas trade—furthering a spiraling decline in Egypt's economy.

As his grandfather had done, Ptolemy IV married his sister Arsinoë, who became guardian and regent of the infant king, Ptolemy V Epiphanes ("God Manifest"). Ptolemy V had been proclaimed joint king with his father within a few weeks of his birth. Fearful of Arsinoë's influence over her son,

Because of the converging empires and their influences, officials in Egypt spoke several languages. The rule of Alexander the Great made Greek the dominant language of government, and the Romans mostly spoke Latin. Cleopatra was the only member of the Ptolemic dynasty to learn the native language of Egyptian, which included hieroglyphics. One of her forefathers, Ptolemy V ordered the creation of the Rosetta Stone *(above)*, which features a royal decree in the three languages of Egypt at the time: hieroglyphics, demotic, and Greek.

however, Sosibus had her murdered. Ptolemy V was not officially crowned until he was 12 years old. Rulers of surrounding kingdoms—especially Macedonia—took advantage of the confused situation in Egypt and established a sequence of regents who ruled Egypt in Ptolemy's name. Ptolemy V married Cleopatra, daughter of Antiochus of the Seleucids—the first of seven Egyptian queens to bear that name—but died at the age of 28, the apparent victim of poisoning.

Ptolemy V Epiphanes, son of Ptolemy IV and Arsinoë, was only a child when he came to the throne; at the time, a series of foreign regents ran the kingdom. Between themselves, Antiochus III, the Seleucid king of Syria, and Philip V of Macedonia agreed to seize the overseas possessions of the Ptolemaic Empire. After several bitter defeats by the Macedonians, Egypt formed an alliance with the rising power in the Mediterranean, Rome. Once he reached adulthood, Ptolemy V became a despised tyrant. When he died in 180 B.C., he was succeeded by his infant son Ptolemy VI Philometor.

The reigns of Ptolemy IV and V marked the beginning of the decline of the house of Ptolemy and Egypt as an empire. Instead of remaining aloof from Rome's problems, Egypt became an official "ally." After the death of Ptolemy IV, Rome sent a "guardian" to Alexandria under the pretext of wishing to "guard" the young king . . . . beginning an interference by Rome in Ptolemaic affairs that lasted until the end of the dynasty. Rome was now free to enter Greece as the protectors of Ptolemy V's territories, repaying their "debt" to Egypt. By the time Ptolemy V died, most of Egypt's overseas possessions had been lost.

Ptolemy V left his six-year-old son, Ptolemy VI Philometor ("Mother-Loving God"), as his heir, with his mother assuming the role of regent. Ptolemy VI was only 15 when she died, and, in the following year, he married his younger sister Cleopatra II.

In 170 B.C., Antiochus IV Epiphanes invaded Egypt, something that had not occurred since the time of Alexander the Great.

During the occupation of Memphis by Antiochus, a revolution took place in Alexandria, which placed the 15-year-old brother of Ptolemy VI on the throne (later, Ptolemy VIII Euergetes II) as a puppet king. When Antiochus withdrew, the brothers agreed to reign jointly with their sister Cleopatra II. They soon fell out, however, and quarrels between the two brothers allowed Rome to interfere and to steadily increase its influence in Egypt. Through the intervention of Rome, Ptolemy VI was returned to the throne at Memphis, beginning a double reign of Egypt that lasted an uneasy five years, with Ptolemy VI constantly quarreling with his brother until his death in 145 B.C.

Ptolemy VI was succeeded by yet another infant, his son Ptolemy VII Neos Philopator. But Euergetes soon returned, killed his young nephew, seized the throne, and, as Ptolemy VIII, soon proved himself a cruel tyrant. He was so grossly obese that he earned the nickname "Physcon" ("Potbelly"). He married his brother's widow, Cleopatra III. He had a son from her previous marriage, Ptolemy VII Neos Philopator, killed. She bore him two sons: Ptolemy IX Philometor Soter II, known as Lathyros ("Chickpea"), and Ptolemy X Alexander I. On his death in 116 B.C., after a 50-year reign, he left the kingdom to his wife and her son Ptolemy IX Philometor Soter II.

Cleopatra III had wanted Alexander to be declared king, but since the Alexandrians refused to consider the idea, Lathyros was brought back from Cyprus, where he was acting as governor, to take the throne. Accusing him of attempting to have her murdered, Cleopatra III deposed Lathyros, replacing him with his younger brother. But Ptolemy X Alexander was exceedingly unpopular with the Alexandrians. The army eventually turned against him, forcing him to flee to Syria. There he raised an army of mercenaries and reentered Alexandria. But Cleopatra III finally tired of her son and drove him out of the city. He eventually came back to murder her. He sold the golden coffin of Alexander the Great to pay for his army, and the outraged citizens of Alexandria again expelled him. Before

Ptolemy X Alexander lost his life in a naval battle in 87 B.C., he had bequeathed his kingdom to Rome—an act that would have horrified Ptolemy I and II. Rome, however, was not particularly anxious to get involved in the current mess in Egypt and instead allowed Lathyros to return as king. He married the daughter of his brother Ptolemy X Alexander I—that is, his own granddaughter. Lathyros—Ptolemy IX Soter II—died in 80 B.C., leaving no heir to the throne other than his nephew, the son of Ptolemy X Alexander I.

The new heir to the Egyptian throne, Ptolemy XI Alexander II, raised as a pampered Grecian prince, became a puppet for the proconsul Sulla, who, by 80 B.C., had become the absolute dictator of Rome. Seeing the opportunity to place a sycophantic protégé on the Egyptian throne, Sulla sent Ptolemy XI to Alexandria. There he took the crown of Egypt and married the reigning queen, his own middle-aged mother,.

Queen Cleopatra Berenice had been left sovereign of Egypt on the death of her father. Accustomed to 20 years of power, which she had to share with no one, she was unwilling to cede control of Egypt to a mere boy. Her concerns reached her son and husband who—inexperienced youngster or not—had Berenice assassinated within three weeks of his arrival in the city. The Alexandrians were so angered by this that they immediately lynched the young king.

There were now no remaining descendants of Ptolemy I other than Cleopatra Selena, the Queen of Cyrenaica and Crete, and those few Seleucid princes who carried Ptolemaic blood.

Two illegitimate sons of Ptolemy IX Soter II were living in exile at the court of Mithridates VI in Syria. One became the governor of Cyprus, and the eldest was pronounced King of Egypt in 80 B.C.: Theo Philopator Philodelphus Neos Dionysus, who dropped the name "Ptolemy" entirely. His subjects referred to him as Auletes ("the Flute Player") or Ptolemy Nothos ("the bastard"), since his mother had been an unknown Alexandrine concubine, depending, apparently, on whom you were talking

Sulla, a Roman dictator who had his opponents in the Senate murdered, placed Ptolemy XI on the throne of Egypt to rule in Rome's favor. After marrying and murdering his stepmother, Ptolemy was murdered by angry Alexandrian mobs, and once again the role of pharaoh was passed on to the closest Ptolemic heir.

to and how they felt about their ruler. Neither nickname suggests that he was taken very seriously, and it is true that he was not very popular.

One of his names, Neo Dionysus (or "the new Dionysius"), was probably meant to be flattering since the god Dionysius was viewed as the promoter of civilization, a lawgiver, and lover of peace—as well as the patron deity of agriculture and the theater. Unfortunately, Dionysius was also the god of wine, whose divine mission was to bring an end to care and worry with the music of his flute. It was this unflattering take on his name that earned Ptolemy the nickname "flute player."

Ptolemy XII, realizing the increasing power of Rome and fearful that it might soon overwhelm Egypt and bring an end to his dynasty, sent a bribe to Gaius Julius Caesar in an attempt to secure his throne, receiving in return the official title of "friend and ally" of Rome. This did not endear him to the Alexandrians at all. When the Romans annexed the Egyptian-held island of Cyprus, the Alexandrians forcibly deposed Ptolemy XII, thereby bringing his older sisters Cleopatra VI and Berenice IV to power. After the death of Cleopatra VI, however, Ptolemy XII, upon payment of yet another massive bribe to the Romans, was reinstated as king. Ptolemy XII immediately had Berenice IV executed.

But it was all too late. The strength of the Ptolemaic dynasty was failing, and the power of the Roman Empire was rising. City after city was falling to the Roman power while the Romans meanwhile gained more and more control over Egypt. When Ptolemy Auletes died only two years after his return to Egypt, the end of his dynasty appeared to be assured. The throne was now up for grabs; Egypt itself was a shattered kingdom. Powerful Rome was about to pounce upon its ruins and absorb it into its ever-expanding empire.

This is the world that the third daughter of Ptolemy XII, Cleopatra VII, inherited.

CHAPTER

4

Julius Caesar

THE YEAR OF PTOLEMY XII'S DEATH WAS MARKED BY A SOLAR ECLIPSE.
Fifteen days afterward, the young queen—a faithful follower of
her father's beliefs—carried out the required rites. According to
an ancient record of the event, a sacred bull was symbolically
crowned by the new king—Cleopatra's brother, Ptolemy XIII.
Cleopatra then led the animal onto a ship surrounded by the
king's boats, where all the people and priests of Thebes and Her-
monthis worshiped it. It was Cleopatra's first public act as queen.

There were no laws regarding succession to the Egyptian
throne. It would not pass automatically to Cleopatra nor to any
one of her brothers and sisters. Ptolemy XII had to specify in
his will who was to rule Egypt after him. Not wishing to deed
the country over to his Roman creditors, he decided instead to

leave it to his children. He had six to choose from, all of whom, he knew, eagerly coveted the throne. He chose his daughter Cleopatra VII, who was his eldest child, and her brother Ptolemy XIII, the eldest boy. They would rule jointly.

So, in 51 B.C., 17-year-old Cleopatra found herself sharing the throne of Egypt with her 11-year-old brother. This was not the ideal situation she would have preferred nor what she had spent much of her life preparing for. However, her father's will stated that his kingdom would be jointly shared by her and Ptolemy—with Rome as their legal guardian, represented by the person of Pompey, a member of the ruling triumvirate. Both law and custom dictated that, in order for her to occupy the throne, she had to have a consort—which could be either a brother or a son. This meant she had to marry Ptolemy—at least in name—so she would be able to rule as queen. In October of the following year, 50 B.C., Cleopatra and Ptolemy were promoted to senior rulers, although because of Ptolemy's age the eunuch Pothinus acted as regent on his behalf, along with two other "advisors," Theodotus and a half-Greek general named Achillas. In the king's name, they made the decisions that dictated the daily operation of the nation.

Cleopatra made it very clear that she considered herself the sole ruler of Egypt. She quickly dropped Ptolemy's name from official documents, regardless of the Ptolemaic custom dictating that her brother would be the senior ruler. She also ordered that her name and portrait would be the only ones to appear on all newly minted coins.

All three of Ptolemy's advisors became Cleopatra's bitter enemies from the moment she ascended the throne. They realized that she meant to be the sole ruler of Egypt, and she realized that Pothinus and his gang meant to seize power as soon as they possibly could. As regent, Pothinus was the king of Egypt in every way but name, a position he very much enjoyed and one he hoped to eventually promote into permanency. He could not do this, however, if he had a rival . . . . and he had one in the intelligent, ambitious young queen. Although, members of the

As Cleopatra ascended the throne, she ordered all new coins to bear her likeness. Her coruler, her 11-year-old brother Ptolemy XIII, was killed after a war with Cleopatra.

Ptolemy family had never hesitated to employ assassination to further their careers, this was not an option easily available to someone in Pothinus's position . . . . and even if it were an option, it would be one that was far too dangerous to attempt.

Fortunately for Pothinus, the Nile failed to flood during Cleopatra's first two years as queen. Without the floods to restore the fertile soil of the delta, crops failed and the citizens of Alexandria faced a serious famine. Rebellion began to ferment among the starving people, and Pothinus and his coconspirators realized that they could take advantage of this. By starting rumors that quickly spread throughout the city, they caused people to believe that the drought was the fault of the young queen. Rumors quickly grew to active hate, and hate flamed into open rebellion.

Cleopatra, meanwhile, had created some considerable ill feeling on her own. By 48 B.C., some of her decisions had already angered many of the powerful court officials of Alexandria, officials

Julius Caesar

Like young Cleopatra, Julius Caesar entered the world of power and politics early. When Julius was 16, his father died and left him in charge of the *gens Julia*, or the Julius Caesar family. Julius's uncle was a politician who favored rule by the electorate, whereas his rival, Sulla, favored rule by the aristocratic class. Control of Rome passed back and forth between the two through bloody battles and political tricks, until Sulla prevailed and declared himself dictator of Rome. This put Caesar in a bad position, especially since he had married Cornelia, a daughter of one of Sulla's enemies. Sulla demanded that they divorce, and, when Caesar refused, Sulla ordered him to be executed. Caesar went into hiding until members of his mother's family, who were strong Sulla supporters, persuaded Sulla to lift the threat. Still, Caesar was not considered a friendly face and so he joined the Army, coming back to Rome only after Sulla's death. He became a kind of lawyer, using his amazing gift of oratory to speak out against corrupt politicians; he also advocated reforms.

Caesar quickly climbed the political ladder, first serving as military tribune, then as an elected representative of the army; he moved higher and higher in position, eventually ruling Hispania Ulterior (modern-day Spain). It was during his post as senior consul of the Roman Republic that he met Pompey the Great and formed an alliance with him. Pompey solidified the alliance by marrying Caesar's only daughter, Julia. It was when Julius was elected proconsular governor of Transalpine Gaul who were already disapproving of having Egypt ruled by a woman. An example of this was when mercenaries killed the sons of the Roman governor of Syria, when he sent them to ask Cleopatra for assistance in his fight against the Parthians. Instead of holding the murderers for trial in Alexandria, where the crime had been committed—which is what her court officials wanted—Cleopatra had them returned to Syria for trial.

(modern-day southern France) that he started the first Gallic War and conquered all of Gaul (the rest of current France, with most of Switzerland and Belgium and parts of Germany—effectively western mainland Europe from the Atlantic to the Rhine) and annexed them to Rome.

Julia died in childbirth, leaving Pompey and Caesar distraught. This event marked a dissolution of the bond Caesar and Pompey had enjoyed. As Caesar's power and land grew, Pompey, then head of the Roman Senate, felt that Caesar was quickly becoming too powerful for his position. Pompey called him back from the war, but Caesar refused to give up his army. He crossed the Rubicon on January 10, 49 B.C. with only a single legion of his vast army, inciting a civil war. Not knowing that Caesar had only a fraction of his vast army, Pompey and his followers fled Rome. Caesar followed them. He confronted Pompey in Hispania, then in Greece, then finally defeated him soundly at Pharsalus, despite being completely outnumbered. Caesar was appointed dictator of Rome and Marcus Antonius—who we know today as Mark Antony—was his Master of the Horse, or main lieutenant. Caesar was dictator for 11 days and then resigned when he was elected back into the consul. Pompey had escaped to Alexandria and Caesar followed him. Pompey was murdered by King Ptolemy XIII, and it was then that Caesar found himself involved in the Alexandrine war between Ptolemy and Cleopatra.

Cleopatra, who was no fool, saw what was happening around her—just as she realized there was little she could do about it. The power that Pothinus, Achillas, and Theodotus wielded—speaking as they did for the puppet king—was too much for her to overcome. She did the only sensible thing she could think of. She fled, with her sister Arsinoë, to neighboring Syria. There she hoped to raise an army that would allow her to return to Egypt and reclaim her throne.

Meanwhile, Julius Caesar became the most powerful man in the world. The triumvirate that had been ruling Rome had collapsed. Crassus had died in a battle in Parthia while Pompey and Caesar fought one another. This conflict resulted in civil war that was won by Caesar when he defeated Pompey at Pharsalus in Greece, in August, 48 B.C.

Pompey, not quite admitting defeat, immediately sailed for Egypt to seek both refuge and help, which he expected to find, since he had been appointed Ptolemy's guardian by the Roman Senate. Ptolemy's advisors, Achillas, Pothinus, and Theodotus, welcomed the Roman leader and his army. . . but in a way that Pompey never expected. Instead of offering to help him in his dispute with the great Caesar, they plotted to murder him. In doing so, they believed, they would gain favor with Caesar, who would, in turn, show his appreciation by helping them destroy Cleopatra once and for all. They also feared terrible reprisals from the powerful new emperor of Rome if they sided with his bitter enemy.

Pompey arrived in Egypt in all innocence. He sent messages to the king expressing his desire to continue Rome's friendly relations with the Ptolemies and Egypt. He and his wife were met at the border by Achillas and a Roman soldier, who invited their new guests to board a boat that would transport them to Alexandria. Pompey's wife didn't trust Achillas and urged Pompey not to accept the offer, however friendly it might seem. Pompey ignored her.

He should have listened to his wife. Moments after the boat set sail, the soldier stabbed Pompey in the back. The body was then decapitated and the head turned over to Theodotus, who wanted to present it to Caesar as a token of Egypt's loyalty to the empire. It was September 28, 48 B.C.

Caesar, who arrived four days later, was, much to Theodotus's surprise, not in the least pleased by the gift of Pompey's head. Caesar refused to even look at it, but instead he took Pompey's signet ring, shedding tears as he did. However much he disagreed with Pompey, he had still been a friend, colleague, and respected opponent on the battlefield. To discover that Pompey had been murdered in such a cowardly, dishonorable, and disgraceful fashion infuriated the emperor. He offered both aid and friendship to all who had been friends and companions of Pompey and who, without anywhere to flee, had been arrested by Ptolemy. Writing to friends in Rome, he said that of all the results of his victory, what gave him the most pleasure was that he was able to save the lives of fellow citizens who had fought against him. Since Caesar had not only arrived in Egypt with 3,200 keenly trained soldiers and 800 cavalry but also 12 soldiers bearing the official insignia of the Roman government, he could exercise his wrath with little fear of resistance from the Egyptians.

Riots followed Caesar's arrival in the city. Ptolemy had fled to Pelusium, leaving the palace open to Caesar, who immediately took control. Pothinus, in a panic, rushed to Pelusium to fetch the young king back to Alexandria, to the presence of Caesar.

Pothinus, the most influential person at the court, began secretly plotting against Caesar. Aware that something was going on, Caesar remained awake for whole nights on end at drinking parties, in order to be certain he was properly guarded. Pothinus openly made himself intolerable, belittling and insulting Caesar both in his words and in his actions. He made sure that the Roman soldiers were given rations of the oldest and worst possible grain, telling them that they must put up with it and learn to like it, since they were eating food that did not belong to them. At official dinners, he ordered that only wooden and earthenware

This nineteenth century engraving illustrates the capture of a town by Julius Caesar's Roman army, using ballistics and catapults.

dishes should be used, on the pretext that Caesar had taken all the gold and silver in payment of Egypt's debt to Rome.

It is true that, in spite of his anger at how Pompey had met his death, Caesar had not forgotten how much Egypt owed. To this end, although Caesar wanted Egypt's legitimate rulers returned to their thrones, he specifically wanted Cleopatra back as coregent. With the country restored to the conditions Ptolemy XII had established before his death, Rome could again legitimately drain Egypt of its wealth—money Caesar desperately needed to support not only Rome itself but also the massive army he was building. Ptolemy XIII had, in fact, owed Caesar

17.5 million drachmas. Although Caesar had previously remitted part of this debt to the king's children, he now demanded 10 million for the support of his army. Pothinus suggested that Caesar should, for the time being, go away and attend to more important matters, those for which Egypt would later be delighted to pay the money. Caesar replied that Egyptians were the last people he would ask for advice.

Caesar believed that the quarrel between Cleopatra and Ptolemy directly concerned the Roman people in general and himself specifically, as consul. After all, it was in his previous consulate that Rome's recognition of and alliance with their father had taken place. He declared that the feuding sovereigns should disband their armies and instead submit their claims to peaceful arbitration.

According to historian Dio Cassius, Cleopatra's case was first argued for her by friends, until she learned that Caesar was something of a lady's man. She then sent him a message complaining that her case was being badly mismanaged by her advocates. She told him that she now wanted to plead her case personally. "She was," wrote Cassius, "then in the flower of her age and celebrated for her beauty. Moreover, she had the sweetest of voices, and every charm of conversation, so that she was likely to ensnare even the most obdurate and elderly man. These gifts she regarded as her claims upon Caesar. She prayed therefore for an interview, and adorned herself in a garb most becoming, but likely to arouse his pity, and so came secretly by night to visit him."

Caesar sent word to Cleopatra that he would be pleased to see her return to Alexandria.

Cleopatra now found herself in a quandary. She knew that Caesar wanted her back in Alexandria, which was the best news she could have hoped for . . . but how could she safely return? Seeing her back in Egypt was the last thing in the world Theodotus and his accomplices wanted. He would have her assassinated the moment she stepped foot on Egyptian soil. She had to devise a scheme that would enable her to reenter Alexandria undetected and alive.

The plan she eventually came up with was so unusual, so imaginative, and so dramatic that it has become an inextricable part of the legend of Cleopatra. Taking with her only her friend Apollodorus the Sicilian, she embarked for Alexandria in a small boat. Unseen by anyone, she arrived at the palace when it was getting dark. Since there seemed to be no other way of getting in unobserved, she stretched herself out at full length in a *stromatodesmon*, or bed sack, and Apollodorus, after rolling up the sack and tying it, carried it into the palace to Caesar as a gift. When it was unrolled, the young queen of Egypt fell out at his feet.

History doesn't record Caesar's reaction to this unorthodox entrance, but it is clear that he must have been fascinated. The girl who fell from the bed sack was not especially beautiful, but she obviously had some quality that appealed to the great leader. Caesar was not only a soldier, general, and politician, he was a scholar, poet, and author who had an enormous respect for intelligence and education. It must not have taken him very long to discover that the 21-year-old queen possessed both in abundance, and he found those qualities—combined with her obvious drive and ambition—to be as attractive as physical beauty. It was not long before the 31-year-old world conqueror was in love.

Even though he was infatuated with Cleopatra, Caesar did not lose sight of his ultimate goal: to return control of Egypt to Rome. To that end, he invited Cleopatra to return to her throne—but in the company of her brother. Cleopatra had no choice but to agree. She realized how powerful Rome was and that Egypt had no chance of defying it. Agreeing with Caesar's offer was the only course open to her. It was less power than she wanted—but it was better than none at all. Her position, at least, gave her some hope for the future.

Ptolemy's motives were similar. Under Pothinus's urging, he agreed with Caesar, but only in order to stall for time. As soon as the general left for Rome, Cleopatra would be assassinated, leaving Ptolemy sole ruler of Egypt . . . with his advisors controlling him from the wings.

Achillas, however, was not as patient as his colleagues. Knowing that Cleopatra was untouchable as long as Caesar remained in Egypt, he decided on a very foolish tactic: He would order the Egyptian army to throw him out of the country.

In November, 20,000 of Ptolemy's soldiers under Achillas's command surrounded the palace, trapping Caesar and Cleopatra inside. Believing that the Roman invader they detested so much was powerless, the citizens of Alexandria joined Achillas's army in attacking Caesar. It was the beginning of the short-lived Alexandrian War. The greatest casualties were parts of the Alexandrian Library, which was burned, along with some of the city's warehouses. Caesar, however, managed to capture the great Lighthouse at Pharos, by which he maintained control of the harbor.

This war did not particularly worry the warrior who had already conquered much of the known world, although it was a difficult one for him to fight with only a small force at his disposal. The first thing his enemies did was to dam the canals, which threatened to cut Caesar off from his water supply. Then they tried to intercept his communications by sea, and he was forced to deal with this by setting fire to the ships as they lay in the docks. This was the fire that, starting from the dockyards, partially burned the great library.

During all of this, Caesar kept the royal family—Cleopatra, Ptolemy, and Arsinoë—and their advisors safely inside and under guard. Arsinoë, however, managed somehow to slip past Caesar's guards. She joined Achillas and proclaimed herself queen and coruler with Ptolemy, a declaration that was greeted with cheers by the rebellious army. Cleopatra was both hurt and angered by her sister's traitorous defection. It was something for which she would never forgive Arsinoë.

Caesar had already been made aware of the schemes being laid by Ptolemy's three advisors, and when word reached him

After catching Caesar's eye by spilling out of rolled-up bed-sack, Cleopatra was allowed, once again, to rule Egypt. Their union created a bond between Rome and Egypt that made Cleopatra one of the most powerful women in history.

about Arsinoë's defection and Pothinus's part in the conspiracy, he had Pothinus arrested and executed. Meanwhile, the remainder of Caesar's army arrived from Syria and successfully put down the insurrection. Arsinoë was captured and imprisoned. Taken back to Rome, she was paraded in the streets as a royal prisoner of war. Ptolemy was later found drowned in the Nile, still wearing his golden armor.

With the death of her brother, Cleopatra became the sole ruler of Egypt. Caesar had restored her position, but in order to maintain it according to Egyptian tradition and law, she had to marry her surviving brother, Ptolemy XIV, who was only 11 years old at the time.

It is perhaps not a coincidence that Cleopatra became pregnant very soon after this—and was not the least hesitant in proclaiming Caesar to be the father. Caesar never denied this claim—which was probably a true one, in any case—probably because he very much wanted a son to carry on his name and dynasty, since his marriage to Calpurnia had been childless. Cleopatra was surely very much aware that this gave her a hold on Caesar.

With the defeat of the rebellious army and the destruction of Cleopatra's enemies, Caesar now controlled Egypt . . . but he had no plans for ruling the country himself. He was willing to entrust that duty to Cleopatra. Although she was still forced to share the throne of Egypt, this was only a minor technicality. She realized all too well that she had gained her position through the intervention of Caesar, whom she knew expected her to be but a puppet ruler operating under Rome's authority . . . but this was a matter she could deal with later. At the moment, there was no one in the world other than Caesar himself who would dare question her right to rule Egypt.

5

Disaster

WHY DID CAESAR GO TO SO MUCH TROUBLE TO RESTORE CLEOPATRA TO the throne? If he had wanted a sycophantic ally who would have agreed to anything Rome wanted, Ptolemy and his advisors would probably have been a better choice. So far as his duty to Rome was concerned, Caesar's only interest in Egypt was obtaining its vast resources for the benefit of Rome. Ptolemy and Company would have gladly sold out Egypt for a pat on the head from Caesar. Surely they would have been a better choice than a headstrong young woman who clearly had ambitions of her own—ambitions that did not necessarily include Rome. Perhaps Caesar still bore a grudge against Ptolemy and his court for the cowardly murder of Pompey. In any event, there was obviously more to his interest in Cleopatra than mere political expediency.

Caesar and Cleopatra embarked on a two-month vacation up the Nile. They stopped in Dendara, where Cleopatra was worshiped as a Pharaoh—an honor Caesar would never be able to enjoy. In fact, Caesar left the boat only once, to attend important business in Syria. A few weeks later, on June 23, 47 B.C., Cleopatra gave birth to a son whom she named Caesarion (Ptolemy Caesar).

Perhaps some indication of Caesar's personal agenda lies in the fact that it was such a short time after she gained the throne that Cleopatra bore him a son. While some historians believe that this was done in order to establish a new Caesarian dynasty to occupy the throne of Egypt, Cleopatra had as much or more to gain from the creation of such a bond between herself and the leader of the Roman Empire.

Caesar returned to Rome in July, 46 B.C., bringing Cleopatra and her brother/consort Ptolemy with him, along with her entire entourage. The ostensible reason for her presence in the capital was to negotiate a treaty between Rome and Egypt.

During celebrations that lasted from September through October, Caesar was awarded many honors, not the least of which was being named Dictator Perpetuus, making him dictator for the remainder of his life. This title even began to show up on coinage bearing Caesar's likeness, placing him above all others in Rome, a position deeply resented by the aristocracy. The fear of Caesar declaring himself king, thus bringing an end to the Roman Republic, grew stronger when a crown was placed on a statue of Caesar. The crown was quickly ordered removed and not long afterward citizens who called out the title "Rex" to Caesar as he passed by them in the streets were ordered arrested. Caesar's response to this did little to endear him to the aristocracy. He ordered that the arrested citizens be released and, instead, had the tribunes who ordered their arrest imprisoned and stripped of their power.

While conservative Republicans grudgingly accepted Caesar's appointment as dictator, they were less enthusiastic about his private life . . . which, unfortunately, was not nearly private enough to suit them. Although already married to a woman named Pompeia, Caesar openly established Cleopatra in his own home. They were horrified to learn that in spite of the fact that Roman law forbade both bigamy and marriage to foreigners, Caesar planned to marry the Egyptian queen. And in the face of his long-suffering wife, Calpurnia, he was already openly acknowledging Caesarion as his son. One tribune, Helvius Cinna, even went so far as to propose a new law that would permit the emperor to have more than one wife. Cinna's overt rationale was that this would increase the chances of the emperor producing sons to inherit his position—and to be able to disregard the old qualification that a son had to be of legitimate Roman descent. This law, if passed, would have paved the way for recognition of Caesarion as his legal heir. Caesar himself presented a bill that would have made Alexandria the second capital of Rome. Fortunately, neither of these proposals was ever even voted on. In fact, their very existence was suppressed by Caesar's successor, Octavius, who knew full well that they bore the mark of Cleopatra's influence.

Cleopatra herself was not helping matters in the slightest. Living in luxury in Caesar's villa in Rome, where she remained for two years, she declared herself the New Isis and had a golden statue of herself placed in the temple of Venus Genetrix—an act of unspeakable blasphemy in the eyes of many Romans who already saw her as presumptuous, promiscuous, and lavish in her lifestyle. Besides, the cult of Isis was in the midst of a heated controversy at that time. In the decade before Cleopatra's arrival, the Senate—dominated by opponents of the cult—had ordered the destruction of all the temples and statues of Isis. But as the cult grew stronger, resistance to this suppression also grew, and by the time Cleopatra arrived the Senate was having a great deal of difficulty in enforcing its demands. She was probably on hand at the dedication of the new Temple of Venus that Caesar had ordered built...with a statue of Cleopatra inside. Since Venus was linked with Isis, this indicated Caesar's tacit approval of the cult.

During his sojourn in Egypt, Caesar had been impressed by the power and authority a ruler gained from the "cult of the sovereign," the belief that a ruler was, in fact, an actual god. Even before meeting Cleopatra, he had started laying the groundwork for such a belief in himself, claiming that his ancestors were direct descendants of Venus. "Thus," he said, "the sacred nature of kings is united . . . with the sacredness of the gods, on whom the kings also depend." In addition to the statue of Cleopatra as Venus/Isis, he had one of himself installed in the Temple of Quirinus. The inscription on it described Caesar as an "unvanquished god." Most of this was done for purely political reasons: in private, Caesar was open about his atheism.

While Caesar may have been enamored with Cleopatra and planned to marry her, the Romans and members of the Senate were not pleased with her presence, as it directly opposed several Roman customs and laws. One of the biggest offenses by the couple involved blasphemy, as Caesar had the Temple of Venus, seen here, built with a statue of Cleopatra inside.

In flagrant contradiction to the Roman lifestyle—which was on the whole simple and even austere—Cleopatra led a life of self-indulgence and luxury—a luxury she flaunted in the face of the Roman public. One story—which is probably true—that inflamed Roman feeling against the Egyptian queen was the rumor that during a lavish party she was challenged to produce the most expensive possible food. In answer, she dissolved a valuable pearl in a cup of vinegar (some say wine) and drank it.

Although Cleopatra apparently did not involve herself in Roman politics, the famous Roman orator, Cicero, seemed to suspect her of this. There had been rumors to the effect that Cleopatra was urging Caesar to move the capital of his empire either to Ilium or to Alexandria. It is probably certain that she was encouraging him to start a campaign against the Parthians, which would ultimately gain the territory of Syria for her son. In an effort to discover if she had any hidden agendas, he visited the young queen and apparently was one of the few men whom she failed to charm. Instead of beautiful and intriguing, he found her haughty and arrogant.

Some of the dislike for Cleopatra was based on the simple fact that she was *Egyptian*—even though her family's roots were in Greece. The prejudice against Egyptians led some citizens to consider her an unfit mate for a Roman consul. Moreover, many were convinced that she had nothing to offer Rome or its relationship with Egypt; on the other hand, she stood for everything they were against.

Romans had a difficult time accepting Cleopatra because they did not believe that the two nations enjoyed equal status. They felt that Egypt unrightfully expected to be treated as Rome's equal partner. While Rome stood to gain greatly from Egypt's vast wealth in gold and grain, this did not raise Egypt in any Roman citizen's estimation. The Ptolemies had incurred enormous debts to Rome—if any wealth was to come from Egypt it was not due to Egypt's generosity but to the fact that Egypt owed this money to Rome. There was no need for diplomatic relationships with Cleopatra, many believed. If Rome wanted Egypt's riches it could *take* them.

Given this, the Roman government and Roman people were incensed that once Caesar began his affair with Cleopatra, he dismissed Egypt's debt and never spoke of it again. Had Cleopatra not won Caesar's affection, Egypt would never have been treated as an equal power with the ability to dicker with Rome over its debt.

Romans also felt that Cleopatra was merely using Caesar to further her ambitions for Egypt itself—to the detriment of Rome. If Egypt were to be considered an ally by Rome, it would share in Rome's ongoing conquest of the known world. That a nation like Egypt, heavily in debt to Rome and with little or no military presence of its own, would ever even be offered equal status with Rome was unthinkable to most Romans.

Still, Caesar steadfastly refused any offer of a crown. However, during this time Caesar was planning a campaign into Parthia, which stood to gain Rome considerable wealth. An ancient legend said that Parthia could only be conquered by a king, so Caesar was authorized by the Senate to wear a crown anywhere in the empire except Italy itself. Caesar planned to leave in April 44 B.C., and the secret opposition that was steadily building had to act fast. Made up mostly of men who Caesar had pardoned already, they knew their only chance to rid Rome of Caesar was to prevent him ever leaving for Parthia.

Caesar's friend Brutus, along with a group of men calling themselves the Liberatores ("Liberators"), began to conspire against Caesar. Numerous different plans for the assassination of Caesar were discussed, but the majority favored killing him while he sat in the Senate. He would be by himself since only Senators were admitted there, and the conspirators could hide their daggers beneath their togas.

On the Ides of March (March 15), 44 B.C., a group of senators called Caesar to the forum for the purpose of reading a

The death of Caesar marked a turning point for the Roman Empire, and a change in political tactics for Cleopatra. Forced to flee Rome, she returned to Egypt and waited before carefully allying herself with the winners of the Roman civil war.

petition written by the senators, asking him to return their power to them. Mark Antony, a Roman politician and general who, as a military commander and administrator, was an important supporter of Julius Caesar, learned of the plot the night before from a terrified Liberatore named Servilius Casca. Fearing the worst, he hurried to warn Caesar. The senators, however, intercepted Caesar before he reached the senate chamber and directed him to an adjoining room.

As Caesar began to read the false petition, Casca pulled down Caesar's tunic and thrust his dagger at his neck. Within moments, the entire group of more than sixty men, including Brutus, struck at the dictator. Caesar tried to get away, but, blinded by blood, he tripped and fell; the men eventually murdered him as he lay, defenseless, on the lower steps of the portico.

The assassination of Caesar sparked a civil war in which Mark Antony, Octavian (later Augustus Caesar), and others fought the Roman Senate for both revenge and power. Fearing for her life as well as that of her son after the murder of her lover and their protector, Cleopatra fled Rome and returned to Alexandria.

The Roman Senate declared immunity for Caesar's assassins. They also decreed that the terms of Caesar's will be carried out and that he was to have a public funeral. At the funeral, held five days after Caesar's murder, Brutus spoke first. But when Mark Antony spoke, he revealed the conditions of Caesar's will, in which he left 300,000 sesterces to each Roman citizen and his magnificent gardens to the people of Rome as a public park. The citizens who had gathered to mourn Caesar, surprised and shamed by this generosity, immediately rioted. Caesar's body was burned then and there in the Forum. The assassins, in fear of their lives, had to flee the city. Meanwhile, Brutus and Cassius began to raise money and an army in Greece, allying with Sextus Pompey, now a pirate chief.

Also, according to Caesar's will, his 19-year-old great nephew, Gaius Octavius Thurinus, was declared his successor and adopted son, and in April, 44 B.C. he arrived in Rome to claim his inheritance. He changed his name to Gaius Julius Caesar Octavianus (later known as Augustus Caesar). Octavian's claim to the throne did not sit well in all quarters—Antony was particularly opposed to it—and so, most especially, was Cleopatra, who rightly considered it a slap in the face. After all, Octavian was not Caesar's biological son, whereas Caesarion was.

The result of Caesar's assassination was anarchy and civil war in Rome. When the dust settled, the empire was divided among three men: Octavian, Marcus Lepidus, and Mark Antony.

6

Mark Antony

CLEOPATRA HAD, FOR A SHORT TIME AFTER CAESAR'S ASSASSINATION, tried to get Caesarion recognized as the emperor's legal heir, but without any luck. Realizing that without Caesar there was nothing to protect her from the wrath of a city who did not like her on principle, she secretly fled to Egypt.

After returning to Alexandria, Cleopatra had her brother and consort, Ptolemy XIV, assassinated, thus establishing her son, four-year-old Caesarion, as her coregent. Ptolemy XIV had been getting old enough to present a threat to her. One thing Cleopatra had always been adamant about: she would never share the throne of Egypt with anyone. Meanwhile, Cleopatra did everything she could to connect Caesarion in the minds of the Egyptian people with his assassinated father, even going so

Mark Antony

Mark Antony (c. January 1483 B.C.–August 1, 30 B.C.) was a Roman politician and general who was originally one of Julius Caesar's most important supporters (he was, in fact, a distant cousin of Caesar's). Antony was an important supporter of Gaius Julius Caesar as a military commander and administrator. During his teenage years, his parents left him free to wander around Rome with his friends. They drank, gambled, and got involved in love affairs. By the time he was 20, Antony was already deeply in debt to the tune of several million dollars by today's reckoning. He was forced to flee to Greece to avoid his creditors.

While there, he took part in several military campaigns in which he distinguished himself by his bravery and skill in commanding troops. It was during one of these campaigns that he first visited Egypt. In 54 B.C., he became a member of Caesar's staff and again proved to be a competent military leader in the Gallic Wars. Unfortunately, his spoiled, self-indulgent personality caused problems wherever he served, which frequently annoyed Caesar. Still, Antony managed to climb in rank, eventually becoming Caesar's Master of Horse after Caesar became dictator of Rome—a position that made Antony Caesar's right-hand man. His intense, faithful, loyalty to Caesar never got in the way of the excesses he indulged in during his daily life, however. At heart a selfish, self-indulgent, crude man, Antony never allowed duty to get in the way of his habits.

Learning of the plot to assassinate Caesar, Antony was too late to intercede. After Caesar's assassination, Antony allied himself with Octavian and Marcus Aemilius Lepidus. Together they formed an official triumvirate to rule Rome. During this time, Antony met Cleopatra and fell in love with her. The triumvirate broke up in 33 B.C. in a disagreement that quickly escalated to civil war in 31 B.C. Fleeing to Egypt, Antony was defeated by Octavian at the Battle of Actium and then later at Alexandria.

far as to erect a huge temple dedicated to Caesar, called the Caesareum. It was one of the most lavish temples anywhere, filled with paintings and statues made of gold and silver, gardens, libraries, and courtyards. To emphasize the relationship of Rome and Egypt, she had the temple built in the Egyptian style.

As the Roman empire reeled under the civil war that raged, following the assassination of Caesar, Egypt suffered from debilitating plagues and famine. During Cleopatra's absence the canals that carried water from the Nile to farmland had been neglected. Harvests were failing from the lack of adequate water. The bad harvests continued from 43 until 41 B.C. She used these misfortunes to excuse Egypt from paying the subsidies that Cassius demanded. Fed up with Cleopatra's obstinacy, he was on the point of invading nearly defenseless Egypt when he was suddenly summoned by Brutus to join him at Philippi.

Trying to secure recognition for Caesarion from Dolabella, Caesar's former lieutenant, Cleopatra sent him the four legions that Caesar had left in Egypt. Cassius, however, captured the legions and Dolabella committed suicide at Laodicea during the summer of 43 B.C. Her plan to join Mark Antony and Octavian with a large fleet of ships after Dolabella's death was foiled by a violent storm.

Meanwhile, Cleopatra carefully watched to see who would finally come to power in Rome following the civil war that followed the assassination of Caesar. After the deaths of Brutus and Cassius and the triumph of Antony, Octavian, and Lepidus, Cleopatra knew who she would be having to deal with.

Octavian returned to Rome with an illness, leaving Antony behind as the one Cleopatra needed to keep an eye on. Her son had gained the right to become king when Caesar was declared divine on January 1, 42 B.C. The main object of the divination was the promotion of Octavian, but the triumvirate were also aware of the aid Cleopatra had offered to Dolabella.

After Antony won the decisive battle of Philippi in 41 B.C., he turned his attention to subduing the East in the cause of Caesar. After his triumphant entrance into Ephesus he proceeded to drain Asia Minor of money, both to provide for his legions and for his own greed.

Antony summoned Cleopatra to Tarsus (in modern day Turkey) to question her about the assistance she may have been giving to Rome's enemies.

Though she had not previously met Antony, she knew enough about him to know what she had to do to manipulate him to her ends. Although he was well known as a soldier, she knew that his talents as a leader and strategist were limited. She also knew that he was an aristocrat, that he enjoyed drinking and women, and that he had an overpowering ambition. Even though Egypt was on the verge of economic collapse, Cleopatra put on a show for Mark Antony that outshone anything Ptolemy Philadelphus could have done. She also wanted to transform what Antony expected to be little more than a political fund-raising event into one that would have religious overtones for her people back in Egypt and its priests.

According to the Roman historian Plutarch, "She received several letters, both from Antony and from his friends, to summon her, but she took no account of these orders; and at last, as if in mockery of them, she came sailing up the river Cydnus, in a barge with gilded stern and outspread sails of purple, while oars of silver beat time to the music of flutes and fifes and harps. Outstretched under a canopy of cloth of gold, dressed as Venus in a picture, and beautiful young boys, like painted cupids, stood on each side to fan her. Her maids were dressed like sea nymphs and graces, some steering at the rudder, some working at the ropes." As always, whenever she made a public appearance, Cleopatra went out of her way to appear in the form of either Isis or one of the goddess's counterparts, such as Venus or Aphrodite.

If this was all in the worst of taste, at least from a Roman point of view, it was bad taste calculated to a fine degree. Antony, the queen knew, was a man of low taste. Aware of his humble origins,

Summoned to Tarsus, now modern-day Turkey, by Mark Antony, Cleopatra attracted his attention by traveling on her royal barge to greet him. Dressed as Venus and lounging on a golden boat with silver oars and purple sails, she set the tone for their relationship, which was known for its opulence and excesses.

Antony very much liked the idea of being lionized not only by a blue-blooded queen, but also by one of the legendary Ptolemies.

The marketplace in Alexandria was abandoned, as the crowds hurried to witness the great sight. Hundreds of people, fascinated by the spectacle of the huge barge, followed it along the banks as it sailed up the Nile to the accompaniment of flutes, the favorite instrument not only of Cleopatra's father but an instrument associated with the god Dionysus and the favorite of Isis. Cleopatra had gone out of her way to make sure that the people got the point: that (as Plutarch described it) "Aphrodite, for the good and happiness of Asia, met Dionysus at a festive reception." In other words, it was not a meeting between a queen and a general but a meeting of gods.

When Antony came on board, he was greeted by vast, brilliant candelabra in all shapes and forms lowered from above. A simple, self-indulgent man, he was no match for either this much spectacle or for Cleopatra herself. She was, she claimed, Venus herself come to feast with Bacchus, "for the common good of Asia." Antony invited her to join him at supper the following night, hoping to outdo her in lavish showmanship—which was an effort doomed to failure from the very start. Both embarrassed and amused by the failure of his own pretenses, Antony joked about it in the only way he knew how: as the honest, coarse, down-to-earth soldier he was. Cleopatra, according to Plutarch, seeing "that his raillery was broad and gross and savored more of the soldier than the courtier, rejoined in the same taste, and fell into it at once, without any sort of reluctance or reserve, for her actual beauty, it is said, was not in itself so remarkable that none could be compared with her, or that no one could see her without being struck by it, but the contact of her presence, if you lived with her, was irresistible; the attraction of her person, joining with the charm of her conversation and the character that attended all she said or did, was something bewitching. It was a pleasure merely to hear the sound of her voice."

Antony, whether he knew it at the time or not, was already in over his head. Just as she had done with Caesar, Cleopatra had conquered another hero. Abandoning his original reasons for meeting the queen, he instead accompanied her to Alexandria where they spent the winter of 41–40 B.C. together.

There—at least according to Plutarch, they spent most of their time in "play and diversion, squandering and fooling away in enjoyments that most costly . . . of all valuables: time." They called themselves and the band of friends who partied with them the "Illimitable Livers" and they lavished entertainments on one another with an extravagance beyond the belief of even the Romans. Plutarch tells of one of Cleopatra's cooks who, when first taken into the kitchen "where he admired the prodigious variety of all things, but, particularly seeing eight wild

Was Cleopatra Beautiful?

This is a question that has been asked over and over again for more than two thousand years. Plutarch states expressly that her fascination did not lie so much in her beauty as in a combination of physical attractiveness and great intelligence.

What did she actually look like? The common misconception is that Cleopatra was Egyptian—but she was in fact a pure Macedonian, a race more closely related to the Greeks. She was more likely to be fair-skinned and blonde—as was her ancestor Alexander—than the stereotyped image of a dark-skinned, dark-haired, dark-eyed beauty. There are, sadly, few contemporary images of Cleopatra. Her profile appears on a number of coins, but they can hardly be counted on as accurate portraits. While we know that Cleopatra was famous for her regal nose, the woman on the coins looks more like an aging Wicked Witch of the West than a girl in her twenties. There are a couple of surviving portrait busts, fortunately, that give us a good look at the young queen. They reveal a girl who was neither ugly nor extraordinarily beautiful. Her nose is prominent—but it seems to fit her oval face nicely enough. It might even be said to be "queenly."

She was probably petite—though no one of her time was very tall—otherwise she would never have been able to have been carried into Caesar's presence.

So how did a rather plain-looking young woman become transformed into one of history's greatest beauties? Probably because until relatively recently most historians, poets, and playwrights were men . . . and men simply could not fathom how a woman could have accomplished all the things Cleopatra did. The only way they could accept a woman triumphing over great men like Julius Caesar was to assume she did it through sex. She won over Caesar and Antony because she was *beautiful* . . . it could not possibly have been because she had a brilliant mind.

boars roasting whole, says he, 'Surely you have a great number of guests.' The cook laughed at his simplicity, and told him there were not above twelve to dine, but that every dish was to be served up just roasted to a turn, and if anything was but one minute ill timed it was spoiled."

What kind of fascination did Cleopatra have over Antony? Plutarch wrote of her that, "Plato admits four sorts of flattery, but she had a thousand. Were Antony serious or disposed to mirth, she had at any moment some new delight or charm to meet his wishes; at every turn she was upon him, and let him escape her neither by day nor by night. She played at dice with him, drank with him, hunted with him; and when he exercised in arms, she was there to see. At night she would go rambling with him to disturb and torment people at their doors and windows, dressed like a servant woman, for Antony also went in servant's disguise... However, the Alexandrians in general liked it all well enough, and joined good humoredly and kindly in his frolic and play."

Still, even among this endless partying, Cleopatra never forgot her true purpose and never missed an opportunity of reminding Antony what that was. A story told by Plutarch shows just how subtle she could be about doing this:

Antony "went out one day to angle with Cleopatra, and being so unfortunate as to catch nothing in the presence of his mistress, he gave secret orders to the fishermen to dive under water and put fishes that had been already taken upon his hooks, and these he drew in so fast that the Egyptian perceived it. But feigning great admiration, she told everybody how dexterous Antony was, and invited them next day to come and see him again. So when a number of them had come on board the fishing boats, as soon as he had let down his hook, one of her servants was beforehand with his divers and fixed upon his hook a salted fish from Pontus. Antony, feeling his line taut, drew up the prey, and when, as may be imagined, great laughter ensued,

'Leave,' said Cleopatra, 'the fishing rod, autocrat, to us poor sovereigns of Pharos and Canopus; your game is cities, kingdoms, and continents.'"

If any proof was needed that Cleopatra had established a firm hold on Antony, it was his obedience to her order that he have her sister Arsinoë killed in the temple of Artemus Leucophryne at Miletus, where she had taken refuge. Cleopatra had never forgiven her for her betrayal during the siege of the palace at Alexandria.

In the spring of 40 B.C., Mark Antony left Cleopatra and returned home. He did not see her again for four years. While he had been dallying in Alexandria, Antony's wife, Fulvia, had been maintaining his dispute with Octavian over allotments of land for veterans. She was forced to flee to Greece, where she had a bitter confrontation with Antony. She became ill and died there. Antony restored his position with Octavian that same autumn by marrying Octavian's half sister, Octavia. She was a beautiful and intelligent woman who had been recently widowed. She had three children from her first marriage.

Six months after Antony returned to his duties in Rome, Cleopatra gave birth to twins, Cleopatra Selene and Alexander Helios. It would be four years before they met their father. Antony and Octavia had two daughters, both named Antonia. She did not waste her time pining for Antony. We know, for instance, that she began work on restoring and enlarging many of the national temples, such as that at Dendera, one of the most beautiful of all of ancient Egypt's surviving structures.

During all this time, Antony never forgot the treasures of Egypt and how much he wanted them. In 37 B.C., he again visited Cleopatra. Octavian had ordered him to lead an invasion in Parthia—where he surely knew Antony would succumb to the nearby presence of the Egyptian queen. Octavia accompanied Antony as far as Corcyra. But, under the excuse of wanting to protect her from danger, he sent her back to Rome. He convinced her by telling her that she would be of much greater value there, keeping peace with her brother, Octavian.

With Octavia gone, Antony rushed the Parthian campaign in order to join Cleopatra—and as a result was soundly defeated by his enemy. As soon as he reached Antioch, he sent for the queen. She arrived with food, clothing, and money for his army. "Flinging off all good and wholesome counsel," says Plutach, Antony presented Cleopatra with territories that were essential to Egypt, including Cyprus, the Cilician Coast, Phoenicia, Coele Syria, Judea, and Arabia. These were gifts that very much annoyed Rome. Egypt could now build ships from the lumber from Cilician Coast—and Cleopatra proceeded to create a vast fleet.

Cleopatra returned home to Alexandria to await Antony's return. On the way, she made a state visit to Herod in Jerusalem. The reunion of Antony and Cleopatra was the last thing in the world Herod wanted, since Antony's ambitions directly opposed his own. Plutarch describes this historic meeting between the infamous monarchs: "The scene at Herod's palace must have been inimitable. The display of counter fascinations between these two tigers; their voluptuous natures mutually attracted; their hatred giving to each that deep interest in the other which so often turns to mutual passion while it incites to conquest; the grace and finish of their manners, concealing a ruthless ferocity; the splendor of their appointments—what more dramatic picture can we imagine in history?"

Plutarch reports that Cleopatra attempted to seduce Herod, but failed due to his devotion to his wife, Mariamne, an attempt that so reputedly so offended Herod that he considered putting the queen to death. He was only dissuaded by advisors who warned him that such an act would bring down a terrible retribution on his head from Antony. "So she was escorted with great gifts and politenesses back to Egypt."

Meanwhile, Cleopatra had a third child by Antony. He married her in 36 B.C., and she gave birth to another son, Ptolemy Philadelphus. Early in 35 B.C., Antony returned to Egypt with her. From then on, Alexandria was his home, and Cleopatra was his life. Nothing about this affair sat well with Octavia,

Mark Antony was under Cleopatra's spell, but could not ignore professional and personal duties back in Rome. During the four years he was away, Cleopatra improved some of Egypt's national temples. The Temple of Dendara features the only carving of Cleopatra still in existence, along with her son, Caesarion.

who decided to travel to Alexandria where she could confront her husband face-to-face. She arrived in Athens with supplies and reinforcements for her husband. Her brother, Octavian, tried to provoke Antony into a fight, sending troops as well as ships to try to force Antony into a war, which by this time was almost inevitable. If Antony had returned to Rome in 35 B.C., he might have been able to heal the breech between himself and Octavia and her brother. Instead, he chose to remain with Cleopatra.

Although unhappy, Octavia remained completely loyal to Antony through all of this. By the time she reached Athens on her journey, she received a letter from Antony asking her to wait in the city, where he would meet her. This was not a meeting that Cleopatra wanted to occur and she did her best to keep him in Alexandria. Determined to keep Antony away from his legitimate wife, she literally had tantrums—even going so far as to go on a hunger strike—until he gave in and canceled his rendezvous with Octavia—who had to return to Rome without seeing Antony.

In 34 B.C., Antony led a campaign into Armenia, which was both successful and financially rewarding. He celebrated this triumph with a lavish parade through Alexandria with the king of Armenia displayed in golden chains. Cleopatra presided as the New Isis and Antony presented himself as the New Dionysus. The procession was a combination of Roman triumph and Egyptian worship of their rulers. It was, by the way, the first time such a Roman victory parade had been held outside of Rome—a fact which angered a great many Romans. Within a few days, a more political ceremony took place in which the children were given their royal titles, with Antony sitting on the throne beside them.

Even with the arrival of her other children, Cleopatra had never given up promoting Caesarion as the sole heir to the throne of Egypt. She had inscriptions and images of him placed everywhere.

The affair between Antony and Cleopatra and the dishonor-able way in which Antony treated Octavia only served to drive the wedge between Rome and Cleopatra even deeper. Even worse was the news that Cleopatra and Antony were calling themselves the New Isis and the New Dionysus. Setting oneself

Cleopatra's Children

You might think being the child of a powerful Queen would be a life filled with extravagance and luxury, but that is far from the truth in the case of Cleopatra's children. She had four children and their lives were not easy. Instead, they were marked with great danger, sorrow, and hardship. She had her first child with Julius Caesar, followed by three with Marc Antony. Cleopatra's own life was constantly in peril as she moved from Alexandria to Rome and back again. The lives of her children were in danger as well; the state of their lives depended upon who was in power, and who was in power in Cleopatra's time was constantly changing.

On June 23, 47 B.C., Ptolemy Caesar was born to Cleopatra and Julius Caesar. He was known as Caesarion, which means "little Caesar," partially in order to make clear that he was in fact, the son of Caesar. There was some question as to who his "real" father was because most Romans did not want Caesarion to lay claim to the Roman throne. However, history considers Caesarion to be Caesar's only son, a fact that Caesar disregarded when he named his grandnephew, Octavian, his successor.

Usually, the eldest son inherited the throne from his father or mother. So Caesar adopted Octavian as his son, in order to declare him his heir. Familial relations and the succession of heirs in ancient times were of the utmost importance. Because kings and queens had such extreme power all to themselves, it was important to the survival of their families that all that power stay within their bloodline.

On December 25, 40 B.C. Cleopatra and Mark Antony's twins, Alexander Helios and Cleopatra Selene (II), were born. About four years later, Ptolemy Philadelphus was born to them. Mark Antony already up as a god went against everything a Roman believed in. In a ceremony held in 34 B.C., Antony deliberately displayed his contempt for Rome. On the exercise ground of the palace, two golden thrones were placed on a silver platform. One throne was for Antony, the other for Cleopatra. At their feet were smaller

had at least four children with his previous wives, including Octavia, to whom he was married when he met Cleopatra. But he abandoned them and devoted himself to the children he and Cleopatra had. In late 34 B.C. Mark Antony gave gifts of territory to Cleopatra and her children, an event known as the Donations of Alexandria. Cleopatra and Caesarion were made corulers of Egypt and Cyprus. Alexander was given Armenia, Media, and Parthia. Cleopatra Selene was crowned the ruler of Cyrenaica and Libya, and Ptolemy was made ruler of Syria, Phoenicia, and Cilicia.

When Octavian invaded Alexandria, Cleopatra sent her eldest son, Caesarion to Berenice, an Egyptian seaport, for safety. He arrived there with his tutor and guardians, but it is unclear what happened next. It is possible that they betrayed him to Octavian and exposed his location. In any case, Octavian had 17-year-old Caesarion murdered out of fear that there were "too many Caesars" and that Caesarion would eventually lay claim to his throne. Though with Octavian in complete control of Rome and now Egypt, Caesarion's control of Rome was very unlikely. And what happened to the other three children? Not much is known about them. After their parents committed suicide, Octavian paraded the orphans around Rome in heavy golden chains in a cruel show of power. The twins were about 10 years old and young Ptolemy only six. Octavian then deemed Octavia, Mark Antony's previous wife, their guardian. And because not much else was recorded about the rest of their lives, it is thought that they did not live into adulthood.

thrones for their children. Antony declared his son Alexander Helios the king of Armenia, his daughter Cleopatra Selene the queen of Cyrenaica and Crete, and two-year-old Ptolemy Philadelphus the king of Syria. Caesarion was proclaimed the "King of Kings," and Cleopatra herself the "Queen of Kings."

Antony left for Athens after this, where "fresh sports and play-acting" awaited him. Cleopatra, jealous of the honors Octavia had received at Athens—where the people loved her—courted the city with all sorts of gifts.

In 32–31 B.C., Antony divorced Octavia. This forced Rome to acknowledge his relationship with Cleopatra. He had already put her name and face on the silver denarii, a Roman coin. But Antony went too far when he declared Caesarion the legitimate heir to Caesar instead of Octavian. In doing this he declared an end to his allegiance to Rome. Octavian decided

to publish Antony's will, immediately stripping Antony of power and declaring war on Egypt. Antony's name was nowhere mentioned in the official declaration.

On the brink of war with Rome, Cleopatra sailed for Greece with 200 warships. While in Athens, she had a statue of herself in the image of Isis erected in the Acropolis. From Ephesus, she continued to Samos in the spring of 32 B.C., where she and Antony took part in a celebration of the cult of Dionysus. "Every city," wrote Plutarch, "sent an ox for the sacrifice and the kings tried to outdo one another with receptions and gifts." Although they gained some support, this bid of Cleopatra and Antony to gain allies in their expected fight against Rome ultimately failed. Antony simply did not possess the charisma that had made Alexander or Caesar so popular, nor did many of the kings accept the divinity of Cleopatra and Antony. Cleopatra was never successful in establishing a cult of her own.

The decision to go to war with Cleopatra was not unanimous, however. A third of the Roman Senate and two consuls joined with Antony. The war began in 31 B.C., when Roman Admiral Agrippa captured the Greek city and naval port of

Methone, which was loyal to Antony. The Roman fleet led by Agrippa met that of Antony and Cleopatra outside the Gulf of Actium on the morning of September 2, 31 B.C., as Antony led 220 warships through the straits. There he found the Roman fleet blocking his exit.

Most of Antony's warships were huge quinqueremes, slave-driven galleys with massive rams weighing up to three tons. These were used to punch fatal holes in the waterlines of enemy ships. To keep themselves from being damaged by a similar tactic, the bows of Antony's ships were covered with bronze plates and reinforced with square cut timbers. In spite of their size and strength, these ships were seriously undermanned. There had been an outbreak of malaria that had devastated Antony's crews as they were waiting for the Roman fleet to arrive. This and the fact that the Romans had cut Antony's supply lines demoralized the crews that survived the malaria. In addition to Antony's fleet, Cleopatra contributed 60 ships of her own.

An experienced general, Antony was no admiral. He was literally out of his depth commanding a navy and was finally forced to burn the ships that could no longer be effectively manned. The remainder he clustered together defensively.

Unlike Antony's fleet of huge, massive galleys, Agrippa's fleet consisted mostly of smaller Liburnian vessels. Nor had his well-trained, disciplined crews suffered the demoralizing effects of disease and lack of supplies. Though smaller, Agrippa's galleys were more maneuverable than Antony's monsters. Since the main Egyptian offensive tactic was ramming, all Agrippa's captains had to do was keep their nimble little ships out of the way of the slow-moving rams—something they found easy to do. They also made difficult targets for Antony's stone-flinging catapults and bowmen.

There was even worse news for Antony. One of Antony's generals, a man named Delius, had defected to Octavian, bringing with him all of Antony's battle plans. Knowing what his opponent planned to do, Octavian kept his entire fleet carefully

The war Mark Antony and Cleopatra waged against Octavian never gained much ground, due largely in part to Antony's shortcomings in commanding a fleet instead of his usual infantry. The battle of Actium *(illustrated above)* is where Antony lost the war; when Cleopatra's ships turned and fled to open sea, Antony inexplicably chased after her with a quarter of his own ships, essentially giving away the battle to Octavian.

out of range. Shortly after midday, Antony was forced to leave the protection of the shore to engage the enemy directly at last.

From shore, Cleopatra saw the tide of battle turn against her lover. Her personal fleet fled the battleground, retreating to the open sea. Seeing that the battle was going against Antony, Cleopatra's fleet retreated to open sea beyond, without firing a shot. Seeing her ships retreating, Antony abandoned his men to follow her, escaping by retiring with his flag to a smaller vessel. Seeing this, the Romans were convinced more than ever that the once-great Antony had been blinded by his infatuation with Cleopatra, unable to think or act on his own. With a few ships accompanying him as an escort, Antony managed to break through Octavian's lines. Those that were left behind were captured or sunk by the Romans. The battle was over.

For three days, Antony sat alone in the prow of Cleopatra's ship, refusing to either see or speak to her. They returned to Egypt, where Antony lived alone for a time, brooding, while Cleopatra anxiously prepared for an invasion by Rome. When Antony received word that his forces had surrendered at Actium and his allies had gone over to Octavian, he left his solitary home and returned to Cleopatra to party away their final days.

The repercussions of the brief, disastrous battle at Actium were tremendous. At the start of the war, Rome believed that Antony, as an experienced, competent military leader could, along with an army as large as Octavian's, present a serious challenge to the emperor. Now the emperor, his generals, and his admirals knew that Antony posed no real threat at all.

Cleopatra began experimenting with various poisons to learn which would cause the most painless death. She also built a mausoleum to which she moved all of her gold, silver, emeralds, pearls, ebony, ivory, and other treasure.

Octavian reached Alexandria on July 31, 30 B.C. Antony marched his army out of the city to meet him. From high ground, where he expected to see a naval battle between his fleet and the Roman fleet, Antony instead saw his fleet salute the Romans with their oars and join them. Already 19 of his infantry legions and 12,000 cavalry—learning of Antony's humiliating defeat at Actium—had deserted under cover of darkness. Antony returned to the city, shouting that Cleopatra had betrayed him.

Terrified that her lover meant to kill her, Cleopatra fled to her treasure house in which she barricaded herself. She ordered her servants to tell Antony she was already dead. Antony believed this when he heard it. Returning to his own apartments, he ordered a servant named Eros to kill him. Eros, however, killed himself instead, preferring death to being the murderer of his master. With no one to help him, Antony was forced to stab himself in the stomach. He passed out on a couch. When he later regained consciousness, he begged his servants to put him out of his misery, but they fled in terror. Finally, Cleopatra's secretary arrived and told him that the queen wanted to see him.

Overjoyed to hear that Cleopatra was alive, Antony had himself carried to her mausoleum. Cleopatra was afraid to open the door because of the approach of Octavian's army, so she and her two remaining servant women let down ropes from a window and pulled the mortally wounded man into her room. Cleopatra laid Antony on her bed and, in despair, begged the man she called her lord, husband, and emperor not to leave her. Antony asked her not to pity him but to, instead, remember his past happiness with her. Then he was gone.

CHAPTER

7

The Last Days of Cleopatra

AFTER ANTONY'S SUICIDE, CLEOPATRA WAS TAKEN TO OCTAVIAN. SHE attempted to negotiate surrender to Octavian on her own terms, but instead, her role in his triumph was carefully explained to her. Unlike either Caesar or Antony, he had no interest in entering into any relationship, negotiation, or reconciliation with the erstwhile Queen of Egypt. She would, he told her, be treated as the prize of war she was. She would be paraded as a slave through the cities over which she had once ruled. She no doubt remembered how her sister Arsinoë had been humiliated that way.

She refused to admit Octavian and his men when they reached her mausoleum. Instead, she tried to bargain with them through the barred door, demanding that her kingdom be divided among her children. Octavian ordered one man to keep her talking while others set up ladders and climbed through the window. When Cleopatra saw the men she tried to stab herself with a dagger, but the men managed to disarm her and she was taken prisoner. Her children were also taken prisoner, though they were all treated well.

Octavian allowed Cleopatra to arrange Antony's funeral—perhaps less out of respect for the queen and her relationship with the once-great man than out of respect for a brave general that all Rome once revered and respected. She buried her lover with all the pomp and splendor due a king. After the funeral she took to her bed, sick with grief. She wanted to kill herself, but Octavian kept her under close guard. One day he visited her and she flung herself at his feet, nearly naked, and told him she wanted to live. Octavian was lulled into a false sense of security.

But Cleopatra was determined to die—perhaps because she had lost Mark Antony, perhaps because she knew Octavian intended to humiliate her, as her sister Arsinoë had been humiliated, by marching her through Rome in chains. With Octavian's permission she visited Antony's tomb. Afterward, she returned to the mausoleum, bathed, and ordered a feast prepared. While the food was being made ready, a servant arrived with a basket of figs. The guards checked the basket and found nothing suspicious, so they allowed the man to deliver it to Cleopatra.

After she had eaten, Cleopatra wrote a letter, sealed it, and sent it to Octavian. He opened it and found Cleopatra's plea that she be allowed to be buried in Antony's tomb. Alarmed, Octavian sent messengers to alert her guards that Cleopatra planned to commit suicide. But it was too late. They found the queen dead on her golden bed, with her maid, Iras, dying at her feet. Her other maid, Charmion, was weakly adjusting Cleopatra's crown. "Was this well done of your lady, Charmion?" one of the guards demanded.

"Extremely well," said Charmion, "as became the descendant of so many kings." And she, too, fell over dead. It was August 12, 30 B.C., and Cleopatra had been only 39 years old.

Later, two pricks were found on Cleopatra's arm, leading her examiners to believe that she had allowed herself to be bitten by a poisonous snake that had been smuggled in with the figs. As she had wished, Cleopatra was mummified and buried beside her beloved Antony.

Although Antony's monuments and statues were torn down after his death, Cleopatra's remained. Plutarch records that she was held in such veneration that her supporters—probably the temple priests—offered Octavian 2000 talents to insure that Cleopatra's statues would remain untouched. Even though Octavian hated Cleopatra, this was a fabulous amount of money, enough to support his army for an entire year, and he agreed. Her monuments were left undisturbed.

Cleopatra's death marked the passing of the last pharaoh of Egypt, and the last independent ruler of her kingdom. The following years of shifting religions and wars led Egypt to be conquered several times, and the country did not gain independence until 2000 years after Cleopatra's reign.

Cleopatra had been the last pharaoh; everything she had worked so hard for crumbled after her death. Egypt became little more than a minor colony within the Roman empire. Under the direct control of the emperor, it was the principle source for the grain that fed the Roman army. Augustus, and the emperors who followed him, took the title of Pharaoh as the Ptolemies had done, along with all the divine attributes that came with the position. In Egypt, as in all the other lands occupied by Rome, the Romans were meticulously careful about not interfering with local religions and allowed the Egyptian priesthood all of its privileges. They even built temples dedicated to the Egyptian gods.

Eventually, Latin gradually replaced Greek as the official language, just as the Ptolemies had replaced Egyptian with their native tongue. In 212, nearly 250 years after Cleopatra's death, Egyptians officially became citizens of Rome, and Egypt as a distinct nation effectively ceased to exist. Most of the wealth that the Ptolemies had accumulated was shipped off to Rome and was lost forever to Egypt.

The spread of Christianity during the first century .affected Egypt, and as Rome began its long decline through the third century, the new religion spread from Alexandria into the most distant regions of the country. Christian tradition holds that St. Mark introduced Christianity to Egypt in the year A.D. 37, founding a church in Alexandria in the year A.D. 40. The Egyptian Christians called themselves "Copts," a word derived from the Greek word Ægyptos.

As the Roman Empire disintegrated, its control over Egypt weakened. During the reign of Emperor Diocletian (284–305), the empire was divided into eastern and western segments; he tried to bring some order back to Rome. Under Diocletian's political and economic reforms, Egypt was split into three provinces. Diocletian also began to systematically persecute Christians, whom he perceived as posing a threat to his authority.

An edict declared in 202 had already dissolved the influential Christian School at Alexandria and forbade all future conversions to the new religion. 1n 303, Diocletian added to this by decreeing that all Christian churches be destroyed, their sacred texts burned, and every Christian who was not employed as a Roman official be enslaved.

By 330, Emperor Constantine I (324–337) was ruling both the eastern and western halves of the Roman empire from his capital at Byzantium, which he had modestly renamed Constantinople (today's Istanbul). Egypt, like Rome, was now part of the Byzantine empire, which was now the seat of both political and religious power.

In 312, Constantine made Christianity the official religion, and by the middle of the fourth century, Egypt had become an almost entirely Christian nation. In 324, the ecumenical council of Nicea made the patriarchate of Alexandria second only to that of Rome. It had jurisdiction over all of Egypt as well as neighboring Syria. By 333, there were nearly 100 Christian bishops in Egypt.

A split eventually occurred between the Copts of Egypt and the empire—which grew from a rivalry between the patriarchs of Alexandria and Constantinople as well as from fundamental religious disagreements—and in 451 the Coptic and Catholic churches officially separated. For nearly 200 years the Byzantines severely persecuted the Copts. Their churches were closed and Coptic Christians were tortured, killed, or exiled. By the seventh century, this persecution, along with the heavy taxes imposed by Byzantium, had fueled a deep hatred for the empire. The result was that when the armies of Islam invaded Egypt in 642, the Egyptians offered little resistance to their new conquerors.

Egypt was now part of the great empire of Islam, where it remained for nearly 600 years. The Arabs were followed by the Mamelukes, who ruled Egypt from 1250 to 1517, finally losing control when Sultan Selim conquered Egypt and made it part of the vast Ottoman empire. And there it remained for nearly three more centuries.

One of the many conquerors of post-Cleopatra Egypt was Sultan Slim I, who battled the mamelukes for power in Egypt. During the Ottoman rule, frequent power struggles between the sultans and the mamelukes combined with recurring famine and plague devastated Egypt.

Napoleon Bonaparte invaded Egypt on July 2, 1798. With his army came scientists and historians who began a systematic survey of the land called the "Description de l'Egypte." Napoleon's scientists made maps, cataloged ruins and artifacts, and discovered the Rosetta Stone, the key to translating hieroglyphics. All of this information was published and made widely available throughout the world. This made the recorded history of ancient Egypt accessible to science for the first time.

Following Napoleon, an officer in the Ottoman army, Mohamed Ali, rose to power with the support of the Egyptian people. Reigning from 1805 to 1849, he was instrumental in beginning the modernization of the nation. This process was continued by Khedive Ismail, a member of Mohamed Ali's family, who came to power in 1863. His greatest desire was to see Egypt become a thoroughly modernized country, an equal to France, Germany, or England. One of his greatest accomplishments was the creation of the Suez Canal, which opened in 1869.

Great Britain invaded Egypt in 1882 and occupied the country for the next 74 years. During all that time, prominent Egyptians such as Mustafa Kamel, Sa'ad Zaghloul and Mustafa El Nahas worked hard to attain independence from England. This was finally achieved in 1922, when Great Britain officially terminated its occupation and Cleopatra's dream of an independent Egypt finally became a reality after 2000 years.

8

The Legacy of Cleopatra

THE RUTHLESS, TREACHEROUS LAST PHARAOH OF EGYPT, A GLAMOROUS and irresistible beauty, a sly, strategic Queen, Cleopatra is surrounded by mystery and romantic legends. But whatever qualities she truly possessed, it is safe to say that she has inspired generations of artists and writers. She has sparked the imagination of everyone from Shakespeare to Cecil B. DeMille.

In fact, most of how modern society thinks of Cleopatra has come from the plays, films, poetry, rock and roll songs, operas, and paintings that have depicted her. She makes appearances everywhere. The great Latin poet Horace called her "the mad queen." Dante Alighieri placed her in the second circle of hell in, *Inferno.* She's inspired poets, from ancient times to modern times, such as Geoffrey Chaucer (*The Legend of Good Women*),

Alexander Pushkin ("Cleopatra"), Anna Akhmatova ("Cleopatra") and Ted Hughes ("Cleopatra to the Asp"). There have been at least three operas written about her and countless paintings and sculptures. Her story was considered so important and compelling that it was the subject of one of the earliest films ever made, a silent version of Shakespeare's *Antony and Cleopatra*, created in 1908. Since then dozens of filmed versions of her life have been made and dozens of movie stars have played her, from Elizabeth Taylor to Claudette Colbert to Vivien Leigh. She even makes an appearance in the Rolling Stones song, "Blinded by Love." Cleopatra was a legend in her own time and she is still a legend over 2000 years later. Of course, being such a legendary

Without any accurate depictions of her personality and character from the era, Cleopatra has long been a woman of legend and myth, whose image is open to interpretation. Here, in Tiepolo's "Banquet of Cleopatra," he paints the Egyptian queen who arrogantly challenges Mark Antony, a famous Roman general and leader.

subject has its drawbacks. Artists and writers have conceived of Cleopatra in innumerable ways, and not many of them have been positive and flattering. No two interpretations of her personality are alike, and none of them can be entirely accurate.

Consider the difference in the portrayal of Cleopatra in the following two paintings. Giovanni Battista Tiepolo painted *Banquet of Cleopatra* in the 1740s. The painting depicts the legendary banquet scene when a blonde Cleopatra dissolves a pearl in a cup of wine in order to win a bet she had with Marc Antony as to who could throw the most extravagant feast. This is Cleopatra at her most arrogant and powerful, outdoing the formidable and famous Roman. Then consider John William Waterhouse's regal and sultry 1888 portrait of her. It is an intimate painting in his Pre-Raphaelite style, a style that usually portrayed more demure women. She is alone, without all the trappings of royalty, such as servants and exquisite feasts, and her smoldering eyes are directed toward something outside of the painting. This portrait portrays a different Cleopatra whose desires are more personal and emotional, rather than cunningly political. She comes to life in Waterhouse's portrait in a way that she does not in Tiepolo's. Waterhouse seems to pull her out of the world of flat fact and history, placing her into a world of a living, breathing legend.

Mestrius Plutarchus, better known as Plutarch, can be credited with founding most of our notions about Cleopatra's personality. Plutarch was a Greek historian and celebrated thinker who lived nearly 100 years after Cleopatra. He wrote a book called *Lives of the Noble Greeks and Romans* at about the year 100. *Lives* is a book of biographies of important Greek and Roman leaders and thinkers. But Plutarch wasn't interested in just writing down biographical facts about these leaders, he wanted to write about their characters and what virtues and characteristics drove them to greatness or to their downfalls. He didn't devote a chapter to Cleopatra, though she certainly deserved one. In fact, none of the portraits in *Lives* chronicle the lives of women, a fact that is not surprising since women were overlooked in many aspects of society in ancient Greece. Plutarch did, however, write a chapter on Marc Antony, and in this chapter we learn a great deal about Cleopatra, or rather what Plutarch thought about Cleopatra.

His account of the pharaoh portrays her as a power-seeking seductress who tempts Marc Antony away from his Roman duties. Plutarch writes of Antony, "If any spark of goodness or hope of rising were left in him, Cleopatra quenched it straight and made it worse than before." Of course, Plutarch doesn't have much information to go on, since there were no biographies written about her in her lifetime. However, there is no evidence that Cleopatra's influence ruled over Antony as fiercely as Plutarch describes. For Plutarch, Cleopatra embodied all the qualities that were considered unfavorable for women to possess: cunning, ambition, lust. And unfortunately, this is the image of Cleopatra that is most common today.

Someone else learned from Plutarch, someone who was to guarantee Cleopatra as a legend and forever symbolize her as a powerful seductress. It was William Shakespeare in his play *Antony and Cleopatra*, which first appeared in 1623 but is considered to be written as early as 1606. Shakespeare read Sir Thomas North's translation of Plutarch's *The Lives* probably about the time of its publication in 1579. He used what he learned in it to write *Antony and Cleopatra*, and it is by far the most famous account, fictional or nonfictional, of her life. Shakespeare remained true to Plutarch, so true that he lifted whole passages from North's translation, with little rearranging, and put them directly into his play. This description of Cleopatra's barge in *Antony and Cleopatra* only slightly deviates from North's translation:

> The barge she sat in, like a burnished throne/ Burned on the water; the poop was beaten gold;/ Purple the sails, and so perfumed that/ The winds were love-sick with them; the

oars were silver,/ Which to the tune of flutes kept stroke, and made/ The water which they beat to follow faster,/ As amorous of their strokes. For her own person,/ It beggared all description: she did lie/ In her pavilion, cloth-of-gold of tissue,/ O'er picturing that Venus where we see/ The fancy outwork nature. On each side her/ Stood pretty dimpled boys, like smiling cupids,/ with divers-coloured fans, whose wind did seem/ To glow the delicate cheeks which they did cool,/ And what they undid did. [...] Her gentlewomen, like the Nereides,/ So many mermaids, tended her i' th' eyes,/ And made their bends adornings. At the helm/ A seeming mermaid steers. The silken tackle/ Swell with the touches of those flower-soft hands/ That yarely frame the office. From the barge/ A strange invisible perfume hits the sense/ Of the adjacent wharfs.

Shakespeare used historic accounts very often in his plays, and *Antony and Cleopatra* is no exception. Samuel Taylor Coleridge, the famous English poet born in 1772, wrote, "of all Shakespeare's historical plays *Antony and Cleopatra* is by far the most wonderful." The play follows the relationship between Cleopatra and Marc Antony from the Parthian war to Cleopatra's suicide. It is a romantic tragedy. And though Shakespeare borrows most of Plutarch's attitude toward the Egyptian Queen, in the end Cleopatra is revealed in a gentler light, as a brokenhearted woman, who had truly loved Marc Antony with all her heart. Like Plutarch, Shakespeare's *Antony and Cleopatra* is based on some historical facts, but the great queen's intentions and desires are products of the artist's imagination. Because of the wild, lasting success of Shakespeare's play, the role of Cleopatra is considered one of the greatest female roles in the world of theater. For many people of our time, Cleopatra's name is inextricably bound to that of Shakespeare's.

Another playwright who took Cleopatra for inspiration was George Bernard Shaw in his play *Caesar and Cleopatra*, which

In the movie Cleopatra, actress Elizabeth Taylor recreated the luxury and extravagance of Cleopatra's Egypt for modern audiences. The movie reignited the public's interest in the legendary leader.

was first performed in 1906. It is considered one of Shaw's first great plays and was the basis of the popular 1945 film version starring Academy Award-winning actress Vivien Leigh as

Cleopatra. Shaw fictionalizes the relationship between Julius Caesar and Cleopatra, and the play begins with their meeting when she was 16, ,a newly crowned queen. Here, Shaw takes some license with the historical facts because Cleopatra met Julius Caesar when she was, in fact, about 21 years old. In contrast with Shakespeare's strong and seductive Cleopatra, Shaw's is spoiled and immature. Cleopatra is seen pouting and throwing tantrums, like this one: "When I am old enough I shall do just what I like. I shall be able to poison the slaves and see them wriggle, and pretend to Ftatateeta [Cleopatra's nurse] that she is going to be put into the fiery furnace." In Shaw's notes to the play, he writes about how he's portrayed Cleopatra, "The childishness I have ascribed to her, as far as it is childishness of character and not lack of experience, is not a matter of years. It may be observed in our own climate at the present day in many women of fifty. It is a mistake to suppose that the difference between wisdom and folly has anything to do with the difference between physical age and physical youth."

The world is still under the spell of Cleopatra's legend as is evidenced in the extreme extravagance of the 1963 epic film version of her life. *Cleopatra*, directed by Joseph L. Mankiewicz, starred one of the greatest female film stars in the world, Elizabeth Taylor. It was also one of the most costly films ever made. Adjusted for inflation for 2005, the film cost over $280 million. The money went toward erecting elaborate sets of Alexandria and Rome, the training of horsemen and charioteers, hiring thousands of extras, and Taylor's salary. She was the first Hollywood actor to receive $1 million for a single picture for her role as Cleopatra. Even her wardrobe budget was the highest for any single film actor: $194,800.

One can say, Cleopatra was even a legend in her own time. Roman senators claimed she was a sorceress; rumors and tales of her expensive tastes and outrageous behavior abounded. Not much has changed today. Cleopatra is still considered a legend, whose character and qualities have taken on a life of their own.

Perhaps the way we think about Cleopatra reveals more about our times and ourselves than is revealed about this ancient leader. She will always embody different qualities to many people, but there is no denying her reign as the final Egyptian pharaoh, her fearless command of nations, or her place among the greatest world leaders. Her true character, however, is destined to be misunderstood by history forever.

CHRONOLOGY

◆ ◆ ◆

100 B.C. Julius Caesar is born.

83 Marcus Antonius, or Mark Antony, is born in Rome.

69 Cleopatra VII is born, the third daughter of King Ptolemy XII Auletes and his sister, Cleopatra V Tryphaena.

58 Alexandrians revolt against Ptolemy XII. Cleopatra's older sister, Berenice IV, seizes power from her father.

55 Ptolemy XII returns to rule Egypt with Pompey and has Berenice beheaded.

51 King Ptolemy XII dies, making Cleopatra and her husband/brother Ptolemy XIII joint monarchs.

51 Later this year, Cleopatra assumes all power, her face alone appears on coins, Ptolemy's name is dropped from official documents.

48 Cleopatra is exiled to Syria with her sister, Arsinoë. She builds an army to regain power of Egypt.

48 Pompey is murdered. Cleopatra returns to Egypt and meets Julius Caesar. They become lovers.

June 23, 47 Cleopatra and Julius Caesar have a son, Ptolemy Caesar, or Caesarion.

46 Cleopatra moves to Rome with Caesarion and her new brother/husband Ptolemy XIV.

March 15, 44	Julius Caesar is assassinated by his senators. Soon after, Cleopatra leaves Rome for Egypt. When she arrives in Egypt, she poisons Ptolemy XIV and names Caesarion her coruler.
April, 44	Caesar's great-nephew, Gaius Julius Caesar Octavianus, later known as Augustus Caesar, is named Caesar's successor.
43–41	Egypt is plagued by famine and poor harvests.
42	Cleopatra meets Mark Antony.
40	Mark Antony returns to Rome before she gives birth to their twins, Alexander Helios and Cleopatra Selene.
37	Mark Antony visits Cleopatra for the first time in four years and gives her the territories including Cyprus, the Cilician coast, Phoenicia, Judea, and Arabia. This gift angers and annoys Rome.
36	Cleopatra and Mark Antony are married, despite Antony's current marriage to Octavia in Rome. Cleopatra and Mark Antony have their third child, Ptolemy Philadelphus.
35	Mark Antony makes Alexandria his permanent home.
34	Antony declares Alexander Helios the king of Armenia, Cleopatra Selene the queen of Cyrenaica and Crete, and Ptolemy Philadelphus the king of Syria. Caesarion is proclaimed "King of Kings," and Cleopatra takes the new title of "Queen of Kings."
32–31	Antony divorces Octavia, thus forcing Rome to acknowledge Cleopatra as his wife and Caesarion the rightful heir of Caesar's. This infuriates Rome and Octavian declares war on Egypt.
31	War begins as Cleopatra and Antony battle Roman ships off the coast of Actium, Greece. Cleopatra flees. Antony abandons his men to follow her. Their men are defeated and their allies side with Rome.

July 31, 30   Octavian reaches Alexandria. Antony, after hearing that Cleopatra has died, stabs himself in the stomach and dies in Cleopatra's arms. Cleopatra pleads with Octavian to allow her and her children to live, but he does not listen.

August 12, 30   Cleopatra commits suicide.

BIBLIOGRAPHY

◆ ◆ ◆

Burstein, Stanley M. *The Reign of Cleopatra.* Westport: Greenwood Press, 2004.

Chauveau, Michel. *Cleopatra: Beyond the Myth.* Ithaca: Cornell University Press, 2002.

Chavalas, Mark W., ed. *Great Events from History: The Ancient World, Prehistory—476 C.E.* Pasadena: Salem Press, 2004.

Grant, Michael. *From Alexander to Cleopatra: The Hellenistic World.* New York: Collier Books, 1990.

Hobson, Christine. *The World of the Pharaohs.* London: Thames and Hudson, 1987.

Quirke, Stephen and Jeffrey Spencer, eds. *The British Museum Book of Ancient Egypt.* New York: Thames and Hudson, 1992.

Rowlandson, Jane, ed. *Women and Society in Greek and Roman Egypt: A Sourcebook.* Cambridge: Cambridge University Press, 1998.

Walker, Susan and Peter Higgs, eds. *Cleopatra of Egypt: From History to Myth.* Princeton: Princeton University Press, 2001.

FURTHER READING

◆ ◆ ◆

BOOKS

Abbott, Jacob. *Cleopatra*. Simon Publications: 2001.

Chauveau, Michel. *Cleopatra: Beyond the Myth*. Cornell University Press: 2002.

Chauveau, Michel. *Egypt in the Age of Cleopatra*. Cornell University Press: 2000.

Flamarion, Edith. *Cleopatra*. Harry N. Abrams: 1997.

Höbl, Günther. *History of the Ptolemaic Empire*. Routledge: 2000.

Rice, E.E. *Cleopatra*. Sutton Publishing: 1999.

Walker, Susan and Peter Higgs. *Cleopatra of Egypt*. Princeton University Press: 2001

LITERATURE

George, Margaret. *Memoirs of Cleopatra*. NY, St. Martin's Griffin: 1998. Novel

Haggard, H. Rider. *Cleopatra*. Wildside Press: 2000. Novel

Shakespeare, William. *Antony and Cleopatra*. Play

Shaw, George Bernard. *Caesar and Cleopatra*. NY, Penguin: 1950. Play

MOTION PICTURES

(This is a list of only the best known of the many great films inspired by the life of Cleopatra and the stars who played her. The Internet Movie Data Base http://www.imdb.com lists more than seventy titles.)

Cleopatra (Claudette Colbert, 1934)

Caesar and Cleopatra (Vivian Leigh, 1945)

Cleopatra (Elizabeth Taylor, 1963)

Cleopatra (TV miniseries, Leonor Varela, 1999)

WEB SITES

Cleopatra VII
http://www.tyndale.cam.ac.uk/Egypt/ptolemies/cleopatra_vii.htm

A scholarly look at Cleopatra's life. Cleopatra on the Web

Cleopatra on the Web
http://www.isidore of seville.com/cleopatra/

A comprehensive collection of Cleopatra information as well as an index of online Cleopatra sites.

Cleopatra's Costumes
http://www.davidclaudon.com/Cleo/Cleopatra1.html

A fun look at all the different costumes that have been devised for Cleopatra. Those from movies and plays are compared to what Cleopatra may really have worn.

PHOTO CREDITS

◆ ◆ ◆

INDEX

◆ ◆ ◆

ABOUT THE AUTHORS

◆ ◆ ◆

RON MILLER is an award-winning author of more than forty nonfiction books for adults and younger readers. Long fascinated by the great—yet often forgotten—heroic women of the past, his half-dozen novels have been devoted to strong female protagonists, including *Bradamant*, the story of the legendary woman knight of Charlemagne.

SOMMER BROWNING is a poet and author whose award-winning work has been published by magazines and prestigious journals nationally. She is also an accomplished songwriter and cartoonist.

ARTHUR M. SCHLESINGER, JR. is remembered as the leading American historian of our time. He won the Pulitzer Prize for his books *The Age of Jackson* (1945) and *A Thousand Days* (1965), which also won the National Book Award. Professor Schlesinger was the Albert Schweitzer Professor of the Humanities at the City University of New York and was involved in several other Chelsea House projects, including the series *Revolutionary War Leaders*, *Colonial Leaders*, and *Your Government*.